ADVENTURES IN ART

ADVENTURES IN ART

ART & CRAFT EXPERIENCES
FOR 7– TO 14–YEAR–OLDS

SUSAN MILORD

A WILLIAMSON   KIDS CAN! BOOK
WILLIAMSON PUBLISHING   CHARLOTTE, VERMONT

**Library of Congress
Cataloging-in-Publication Data**

Milord, Susan.
    Adventures in art: art and craft experiences for 7- to 14-year-
olds/Susan Milord.
      p. cm.
    Includes index.
    Summary: Instructions for 100 art and craft activities,
including printmaking, animal art, portraiture, sculpture,
architecture, wearable art, and much more. Provides cultural and
historical information for various items and technologies.
    ISBN 0-913589-54-3 (paper):
    1. Handicraft—Juvenile literature. |1. Handicraft.| I. Title.
TT160.M494 1990
745.5—dc20   90-39031
                                        CIP
                                        AC

Cover design: Trezzo-Braren Studio
Book design: Susan Milord
Illustrations: Susan Milord, with selected
works from the Dover Pictorial Archival
Series
Typography: Superior Type

Williamson Publishing Co.
P.O. Box 185
Charlotte, Vermont 05445
(800) 234-8791

Manufactured in the United States
of America

10 9 8

Notice: The information contained in this
book is true, complete and accurate to the
best of our knowledge. All recommendations
and suggestions are made without any
guarantees on the part of the author or
Williamson Publishing. The author and
publisher disclaim any liability incurred
in connection with the use of this
information.

Susan Milord is also the author of *The Kids' Nature Book: 365
Indoor/Outdoor Activities and Experiences.*

Selected illustrations taken from the following books:

Authentic Chinese Cut-Paper Designs
Edited and arranged by Carol Belanger Grafton (Dover Publications,
Inc., 1988)

The Book of Signs
Rudolf Koch (Dover, 1955)

**The Cornucopia of Design and Illustration for Decoupage and Other
Arts and Crafts**
Edited by Eleanor Hasbrouck Rawlings (Dover, 1984)

1800 Woodcuts by Thomas Bewick and His School
Edited by Blanche Cirker (Dover, 1962)

North American Indian Designs for Artists and Craftspeople
Eva Wilson (Dover, 1984)

Ready-to-Use Old-Fashioned Animal Cuts
Edited by Carol Belanger Grafton (Dover, 1987)

Ready-to-Use Old-Fashioned Illustrations of Children
Edited by Carol Belanger Grafton (Dover, 1989)

The Styles of Ornament
Alexander Speltz (Dover, 1959)

Symbols, Signs & Signets
Ernst Lehner (Dover, 1950)

2001 Decorative Cuts and Ornaments
Edited by Carol Belanger Grafton (Dover, 1988)

For Angus

It has been a special pleasure working with both Susan and Jack Williamson again. They, along with Melissa Masnik, have helped shape this book, guiding and encouraging me throughout its making. I thank them for all their help.

I would also like to thank the many librarians who welcomed me to their libraries. Joy Putnam of the Canaan Elementary School library, Louise Cady of the Canaan Town Library, Mary Gove of the Grafton Town Library, and Connie Tobey of the Gale Memorial Library in Laconia were especially helpful.

Thanks also to Mary Ellen Mac-Coy, Sara Goodnow, Joe Gelbard, R.P. Hale, Lorraine Clough, Betsy Denzer, and Francesca Fay. Their contributions are much appreciated.

I am also very grateful for all my husband, Skip Gorman, and our son, Angus, put up with during the making of this book. Our kitchen resembled an art studio more often than not. Lastly, a special thank you to my father, Jerry Milord, who might be said to have started it all, instilling in me a love of art.

CONTENTS

HOW TO USE THIS BOOK

Here's a book for everyone who loves to draw, paint, cut and paste paper, sculpt, construct...in short, create! There are 100 fabulous art adventures for rainy days, sunny days, and all those days in between.

Take a moment to read these next few pages so that you can make the most of your adventures. Then jump right in anywhere and let the fun begin!

ART FOR ALL AND ALL FOR ART

People have been making art since the beginning of time. It seems to be a very human need. Art is sometimes used as a way to express feelings and ideas; it's also one way to add a little beauty to our world. Of course, some art is made just because it's so satisfying making something with your own two hands, besides being a lot of fun! Whatever the reasons, the creation of art has a long history, and a bright future.

Adventures in Art is for everyone who would like to join in on the fun of creating art. It is bursting with 100 projects you can do by yourself or with your family and friends. There's lots of "fine art"—the kind you'd be proud to hang on your walls—and plenty of craft projects (sometimes called "popular art") to use and to wear. Many of the projects use techniques (originating in different countries throughout the world) that have been handed down over the centuries, but can be made with everyday materials available today.

Adventures in Art is divided into eleven sections, each having to do with a particular type of art. *Paper Capers,* for instance, is full of projects using that all-important art material— paper. You'll find out how to cut, emboss, and bind all sorts of different types of paper, as well as how to make your very own!

The other sections are just as much fun. *The Portrait Gallery* invites you not only to paint a portrait of yourself, but to create an imaginary portrait in the form of a mask. *Lay of the Land* includes painting outdoors, as well as creating a landscape of sorts (you might call it a terrarium) indoors. And there's lots more!

You'll encounter many different art techniques in this book, too, which you can use to

A painting is a poem without words.
Latin proverb

WRAPPED UP

Art is a wonderful thing to share with others. Paintings and drawings, useful items such as scarves and piggy banks, as well as kites and Tangrams, make great gifts for family and friends. You'll find lots of ideas for gift-giving in this book.

There are gifts to delight those who enjoy gardening (a topiary bird makes an unusual present), as well as those who love nature (give a bird house as a gift, and you're giving a gift to nature, too!). Anyone who enjoys making things would certainly find a colorful smock useful.

There are also many things you can craft to make holidays and special occasions more festive and meaningful. Start a tradition of hanging a heart basket full of flowers on someone's doorknob each May Day; at your next birthday, let each guest make his own Tumblebug to play with and then take home as a party favor. Spread joy with art!

10

Artist's Profile
One of the best known Japanese printmakers was Hokusai, an artist who lived from 1760 to 1849. He made nearly 50,000 different prints and drawings in his lifetime. His styles and methods changed so much over the years that he signed his art with over 31 different names. The last name he chose for himself was Gwajyō Rōjin—"old man crazy about painting"!

give these projects your own special touch and to experiment with on your own. You'll have lots of fun discovering ways to use colored pencils, making three-dimensional objects from paper without scissors or glue, and dyeing wool with plants. There are hints for making your drawings more realistic (from still lifes to landscapes) and for modeling with everyday materials that can be air-dried or "fired" in an oven.

You'll also find lots of tricks artists use to make things easier (such as the best way to fold paper and a speedy method for cutting paper tiles for mosaics), as well as fascinating historical facts, artist profiles, and words of wisdom to inspire you. With all this, you're well-equipped for some real adventures in art! Enjoy!

STOCKING UP

Part of the fun of creating art is working with all the different materials available to artists. While some projects are best made with a specified type of paper or glue, there's a lot of leeway when it comes to choosing art supplies.

You probably already have many of the materials called for in *Adventures in Art*. Check at home for white glue, crayons, plain white paper, corrugated cardboard, and leftover bits of yarn and fabric. In fact, it's a good idea to save a number of everyday items that might come in handy in the future. Here are a few suggestions to get you started.

Paper—everything from newspaper to wrapping paper, scrap paper, and old greeting cards

Egg cartons

Milk cartons

Small jars

Cardboard—from corrugated boxes to oatmeal boxes and the backs of pads of paper

String and yarn

Fabric scraps—from old clothing to felt pieces

Buttons, beads, sequins, and other notions

Wood scraps

Popsicle sticks

Wooden spools

Wire, in various sizes

Pine cones, feathers, lichen, bark, and dried flower seed heads

What you don't already have at home can be bought. Basic art supplies can be found most everywhere, including many department stores and supermarkets. There you'll find tape, glue, crayons, markers, construction paper, typing paper, and poster board, as well as a limited selection of paints and inks.

For a larger selection and for better-quality materials, check out an art store in your area. You'll find printing supplies, X-acto knives, art papers (many of which sell by the single sheet), plus a full range of pencils, pens, and paints. Ask a salesperson to help you find what you need. Some things, such as brushes and paints, come in two grades—student and professional. You can save money by choosing the student-grade supplies.

Do what you can to get the most out of your art materials. Use both sides of the paper when you're sketching. Save any usable scraps of colored and printed paper—paper mosaics and collages can be made with the smaller pieces. Be sure to replace the tops on markers and tubes of paint when you're done with them. Always carefully plan any projects that call for expensive materials, so that you are sure not to waste any.

Wood fibers were first used to make paper in the 18th century. A French naturalist studying the way wasps make "paper" from chewed wood got the idea for using small particles of wood for paper pulp.

SAFETY CHECK

Most of the art materials called for in this book are perfectly safe to use. There are a few potentially dangerous materials and tools, however, that you must handle with extra care. Have an adult help you if you are unsure how to use a tool or if you're handling tricky substances.

Most of the projects that require glue recommend using white glue, but a few specify rubber cement. Rubber cement should be used with extreme care. It is flammable, which means you should store it and use it away from any heat source. Its vapors are harmful, so always use rubber cement in a well-ventilated area and cover the container tightly when you are done.

Spray paints and fixatives should also be used with caution. Spray them outdoors whenever possible. Place the object to be sprayed in a large box (this prevents your spraying the surrounding area with the paint). Avoid breathing the vapors.

Protect yourself and your clothing from those inks, paints, and dyes that stain. You'll find the instructions for a simple smock on page 142; wear it, an old shirt, or another smock or apron whenever you are working with messy materials. Wear rubber gloves to protect your hands from dyes, which readily stain skin (don't worry—dyes *do* eventually wash off!).

Handle all cutting tools with extreme care. Linoleum cutting tools are very sharp—use them properly, as described on page 38. Be very careful whenever you are using an X-acto knife. Concentrate on what you are doing, and take your time. Accidents usually happen when you're feeling rushed or frustrated. Read the pointers on page 30 for some valuable tips that will make cutting with an X-acto knife much easier.

Several projects in this book require a stove. Have an adult help you at the stove, if you aren't familiar with it or aren't allowed to use it by yourself yet. Use a potholder when you're handling hot pots and pans. Be especially careful when melting paraffin (it's flammable) and working with hot wax (a project where an adult's help is especially important).

The ideal artist's studio is lit with natural light from high, north-facing windows. The light coming from such windows doesn't create distracting shadows and doesn't have the glare of direct sunlight.

Did you know?
The word portfolio is a shortened version of *portafoglio,* an Italian word meaning "carry sheets" (as in paper).

ROOM OF ONE'S OWN

You don't really need a special room for working on art projects. Most projects can be done at the kitchen table (not right before a meal!) or at a table or desk in your room, if you have one.

It is nice, however, if you can arrange to make a little work area where you can store some of your art supplies near your table. Maybe you can set up in a corner of a family room, or in a little-used room such as a guest room or formal dining room. Getting permission to do so will probably hinge on your keeping your work area nice and neat (and possibly removing all traces of activity whenever the room is needed!).

Use a free-standing bookshelf to hold supplies, or rig your own storage system from cardboard

boxes and other containers. Small sturdy boxes with separate lids such as tomato boxes (ask for these at your market) can be stacked one on top of the other to make the most of a small space. Paint the outsides of the boxes or cover them with paper, to make the boxes nicer to look at. You can also color-code them so that you know what's where.

A bulletin board is nice to have to pin inspirational pictures and works-in-progress on. If you can't get a cork board, improvise and make your own from corrugated cardboard. Ask the manager at an art store if you can have one of the empty boxes that mat or illustration board comes in. These large, flat cardboard boxes are easily pierced with pushpins and thumb tacks. Hang the box on the wall or on the back of a door, or prop it up on the floor near your table.

These same boxes can be used to store flat artwork. Seal up the open end (usually a narrow end is opened) and slit open one of the long sides. This makes it easier to store pictures side by side, and prevents the artwork from getting lost at the far end of the box. Store the box flat. Stack several on top of one another to make your own flat file.

A simple portfolio is another good place to store flat artwork. Make your own from two pieces of corrugated cardboard or foam-core board. Join two pieces (the same size) on one side with strips of wide tape such as duct tape or packing tape. Poke some holes at the top of both boards, thread some strong string through the holes, and tie the string together to keep the portfolio shut. It is best to store this portfolio flat, too, but if you need to store it upright, wedge it tightly behind a piece of furniture so that the artwork inside doesn't bunch up and get wrinkled.

ON DISPLAY

With all the artwork you're making, there will be plenty to put on display. You may want to frame some pieces to hang on a wall. Three-dimensional items such as sculptures can also be given special treatment for display.

Having art framed by a professional framer is expensive. It's much less expensive, and a lot easier, to use ready-made frames. These come in lots of different styles in various standard sizes. In fact, when you want to give a framed drawing or print as a gift, for instance, you might consider buying a frame first, and limiting your artwork to its size.

Most artwork is matted before it is placed in a frame. The mat helps protect the artwork by keeping it from touching the glass of the frame. The mat also helps

set off the artwork, giving it a "finished" look. To mat a picture, use an X-acto knife to cut a piece of mat board the same size as the inside dimensions of the frame. Cut a window in the center of the mat, large enough to show all but the very edges of your artwork. (Cut the window smaller if you want less of the artwork showing.) Use an uncut piece of mat board or sturdy cardboard (the same size as the first piece of mat board) to place behind the artwork.

Of course, you can simply mat artwork instead of framing it. Protect the art itself with a piece of clear acetate sandwiched between the art and the window of the top mat. Or wrap the entire mat with acetate, taping it at the back.

You can also make your own frames. Instructions for two different types of frames can be found starting on page 139.

Sculptures and other three-dimensional pieces can be displayed on table tops or shelves (or hung from the ceiling in the case of mobiles). You may want to make a base for smaller sculptures such as the Kachina figures or salt dough sculptures. A scrap of wood sanded free of splinters and perhaps stained a darker shade is one possibility. Be sure to glue a piece of felt on the underside of the base to protect fine furniture from scratches.

Acetate is available at art stores. It comes in several thicknesses and finishes (clear or frosted). Frosted acetate can be painted and drawn on with water-based paints and inks, too.

VIEWING HOURS

At some point, you'll probably accumulate too many pieces of artwork to have on permanent display. This is when it's fun to set up a "gallery" or "museum" and display some of your work for a limited time.

This is even more fun when you join with other family members or some of your friends to stage a "group show." Turn a room in your house into a gallery or put on an outdoor show. Use freestanding boxes (the big appliance boxes are especially nice) to set sculptures on, or to tape or pin drawings, paintings, and prints to. Outdoors, you can hang art from a clothes-

line or from some rope stretched between two trees.

Advertise the art show and invite all your friends to come and see it. You can even sell your artwork, if you like. People enjoy beautiful things in their homes, and art lasts a lot longer than lemonade!

Probably the most famous painting in the Western world is the portrait known as the *Mona Lisa*. Leonardo da Vinci painted this portrait of a smiling woman in 1503. She is thought to be Lisa del Giocondo, the wife of an official of Florence. It is said that she was entertained by musicians while she posed. Do you suppose that's why she's smiling?

All great art is the work of the whole living creature, body and soul, and chiefly of the soul.
John Ruskin

PAST, PRESENT, & FUTURE

You can create art without ever seeing examples of what other artists have done. But art is something people have been making for a very long time, and there's so much to see!

Where can you find examples of art to look at? Just about everywhere! Museums are one place to go to see what has been done before. There may be a museum devoted entirely to art near you, or one with displays of art and artifacts from your town or region. You'll discover artists who worked in some of the styles and with some of the materials mentioned in this book. Up close, you can see how an artist used brushstrokes to suggest clouds in the sky or the wind rustling through trees. You'll get a chance to see how the arrangement of objects in a still life affects a painting, and how bright and pale colors can be used for different effects.

You can also view paintings, sculptures, and prints first-hand at an art gallery. Generally, you'll find contemporary (recent) work at most galleries, but many artists working today use the same centuries-old techniques.

Art reproductions offer another way of looking at paintings and prints. One place you can look for reproductions is your local library. Did you know you can borrow to take home any framed reproductions they have if you have a library card?

Libraries, of course, are also the place to go to borrow art books. The children's section should have some you'd enjoy, but check the adult shelves for an even greater selection. There are hundreds of art books, many with color pictures of every imaginable type of art, from African tribal masks to zoo art (one way of saying pictures of animals!). You'll also find lots of instructional books you can turn to, if you'd like to know more about figure drawing, for instance, or how to paint with watercolors or oil paints.

TIME FRAME

You'll find the chart on the following page helpful when you need to have some idea how long a particular project takes to complete. These are just general guidelines, of course, because not everyone works at the same rate. It's also impossible to time creativity!

These time amounts are for completing projects once you've gathered all the necessary materials together. Allow extra time if you need to construct a loom, for instance, or make a plant press or a batch of salt dough. Read through the instructions for each project from start to finish, to get a better idea of what's involved. Most, as you can see, can be completed within two hours. In fact, many of the projects that need to dry for several days can also be made in a matter of hours (papier-mâché typically needs the most drying time).

TICK TOCK

Note These times include drying time. The actual artist's time may be much less.

A WORD TO PARENTS

> Every genuine work of art has as much reason for being as the earth and the sun.
> Ralph Waldo Emerson

From the first scribbles made by a determined toddler, to the portraits of his family and the imaginative playthings constructed from wood scraps that come later, a child's art is an extension of himself. With the most basic materials, a child can share with others a little bit of his world, as he sees it.

Adventures in Art encourages children to continue, as they grow older, to share their vision through art. It addresses the interests of children from about 7 to 14 years of age, years when kids are looking for forms of self-expression, as well as showing an interest in "usable" art, such as kites and things to wear. Making art is nothing new, of course; this book offers a variety of media and artistic styles that have been handed down over the centuries, but are as relevant today as ever. *Adventures in Art* is more than just a collection of "things to do." It's an open invitation to discover both the "fine arts" as well as the "popular arts" or crafts that are universal avenues of artistic expression. Many countries and cultures are represented.

There are detailed instructions for 100 projects in this book plus lots of practical pointers for using a variety of materials and methods. Many of the projects suggest variations, offering choices as well as opportunities for self-expression. While some children feel more comfortable following instructions to the letter, others are more inclined to loosely interpret certain steps. There are no hard and fast rules in art, so encourage your young artists to experiment.

If you need some idea how long a project takes to complete, see the chart on page 15. There's no way to time the creative process, however, so these are loose estimates.

Please note that some of the tools and materials should be used under adult supervision; younger children will need you to actually help them. Be sure your children know to ask for help when using sharp tools (such as linoleum cutting tools and X-acto knives), when heating things on the stove, and when melting paraffin and pouring it into molds for candlemaking. Show your children how to use rubber cement properly (always in a well-ventilated area) and how to handle spray paints and fixatives.

Adventures in Art is certainly a book older children can use on their own, but don't let that keep you from lending a hand or make you shy about joining in. You may not consider yourself artistic, but you probably possess many skills you can share with your budding artists. You may have a good color sense or know something about flowers. You may be handy with a hammer and nails or be confident in your sewing. These, and many other skills, make you the perfect partner for many of the activities in this book. Making art at home is a wonderful way for families to spend time together.

Your enthusiasm, combined with the books you bring home from the library, the trips you plan to museums and art galleries, and the wall space you clear for the ever-changing gallery in your own home, will go a long way to providing your children with a lifetime love for art and a confidence in their abilities to create art of their own. After all, as Henry James once said, "It is art that *makes* life."

THE
ADVENTURES
BEGIN

PAPER CAPERS

If there's one material artists use more than anything else, it's paper. While a lot of paper is used for drawing and painting on, it is perfect for crafting everything from cut-paper designs to books. Paper is inexpensive, readily available, recycleable, and comes in a rainbow of colors.

PAPER PRIMER

It's easy to make new paper from old paper. Recycle newspapers, grocery bags, colored construction paper, even old homework you don't need to save, to make distinctive one-of-a-kind sheets of paper.

HANDMADE PAPER

Any old paper that isn't shiny, such as newspaper, computer printout paper, old envelopes, egg cartons, construction paper
Blender or beater
Plastic dishpan (see *Note*)
Mold and deckle (see page 20)
Paper towels
Sponge

Note If you don't have a dishpan, you can use the kitchen sink. Just make sure you strain out all the leftover pulp, before you drain the water out of the sink.

1. Tear the paper into small pieces and soak in water overnight. (Use boiling water and the paper only needs to soak 2–3 hours.)

Turn old paper into new art treasures! Some other ideas for using old paper include masks (see pages 76–77), beads (page 152), and bowls (page 129).

2. Blend or beat a small handful of paper with 2–3 cups of water. Add more water, if the blender seems to be laboring. Empty the pulp into the dishpan. Continue making pulp in small batches. Add enough water to the dishpan, so that when you stir the water with your fingers you can hardly feel the pulp. The water should be about 6″ deep.

3. Stir the pulp well. (Do this before making each sheet of paper.) Hold the mold and deckle together and sink them vertically into the dishpan.

Tilt the mold so that it lies horizontally under the surface. Lift the mold straight up and give it a gentle shake from side to side, and from front to back.

4. Let the water drain into the dishpan. Tilt the mold slightly to help the water run off.

5. Remove the deckle and place the mold paper-side down on a paper towel. Press a sponge all around the mold's screen, wringing out the water as necessary. Lift off the mold.

The Story of Art
The Chinese were the first to strain a pulp made from plant fibers through a sieve-like frame to make paper. They invented this method around 105 A.D. From China, papermaking spread to Japan and other countries in the Orient.

Papermaking was not introduced to the Western world until several centuries later. The first to learn of it were the Arabs who held some Chinese prisoners captive in 751. Eventually the know-how spread to other countries via the Moors. By 1276, papermaking was practiced in Italy and, soon after, in other European countries.

►

Paper made with plant parts generally needs to be dried under weights. Layer the handmade sheets of paper between clean sheets of scrap paper placed between several thicknesses of newspaper. Place a flat board on top and weight with bricks, rocks, or heavy books.

6. Hang the paper towel to dry. The handmade sheet of paper will stick to it. When the paper is dry, gently pull the sheet of paper away from the paper towel.

Tip Experiment with different combinations of paper. Add a handful of small colored paper pieces or flower petals and leaves to the pulp, after it has been blended. Add a few drops of perfume or cologne to the pulp to make scented paper.

MOLD & DECKLE

To form sheets of paper, you need a mold and deckle. These are simply two wooden frames of equal size. The mold has a wire screen or mesh stapled to it; the deckle does not.

Make your own mold and deckle from wood scraps (have a lumberyard rip a 1″ × 3″ pine board in half; cut it into 4 pieces and screw them together at right angles with corner braces or irons), or use 2 old picture frames (remove the glass first).

Just make sure your mold and deckle can fit easily into the dishpan that holds the pulp.

Once you have the frame for the mold, staple or tack a piece of aluminum screen in place. Use masking tape to bind the cut edges. Experiment with different materials for the screen. Finer mesh, such as silkscreen mesh or loosely-woven fabric, makes finer textured paper. Wet the fabric before stretching it over the mold to keep it from sagging too much under the weight of the pulp.

Tip You might want to make sheets of paper that fit in store-bought envelopes when folded in half. When you're making the mold and deckle, keep the *inside* dimensions in mind. The inside area determines the overall size of the handmade sheets of paper.

The more pulp you have in the dishpan, the thicker the sheets of paper. Three whole sheets of newspaper make 15–20 6″ × 8″ sheets of handmade paper, depending on the pulp to water mix. Add more water to the pulp in the dishpan, if the sheets seem too thick.

Make round sheets of paper with an old embroidery hoop. Just stretch fabric between the hoops and proceed as usual.

Our English word, paper, comes from *papyrus,* the name for both the plant and the product developed by the Egyptians around 1500 B.C. Strips of the inner fiber of *Cyperus papyrus* were laid over one another and flattened by beating. Muddy water from the Nile held the papyrus together like glue.

CLIP ART

Intricate cut-paper designs are surprisingly simple to make. These examples are based on traditional Polish designs called *wycinanki* (vi-chee-NON-kee). The first is a symmetrical design made with a sheet folded in half; the second is a circular design similar to paper snowflakes.

SYMMETRICAL CUT–PAPER DESIGN

Thin, colored paper, about 8½″ × 11″
Pencil
Scissors
White paper
White glue

1. Fold the paper in half length-wise, colored-side in. Draw your design on the paper. Use the traditional Polish design shown here or make up your own.

Keep in mind that the folded part of the paper forms the center of the design, when the paper is opened up. (It may help you to think of your design as one-half a design.) Notice how the design is one connected piece. Lightly shade in the portions you want to cut away to make it easier to see your design clearly.

2. Carefully cut out the design. First cut out the main shape. Then cut out any interior sections. Lastly, add the details such as the scalloped edge around the tree. Add more finishing touches, such as veins in the leaves, by folding each leaf section in half and snipping a tiny pattern in it.

3. Open up the paper and glue it to a white sheet of paper. This really makes the design stand out. If you like, frame the design by gluing the white paper to a slightly larger sheet of colored paper.

Tip A variety of fringes can be cut in the folded paper. Make the cuts slightly wedge-shaped, so that the fringe is delineated when the paper is opened up flat.

CIRCULAR CUT–PAPER DESIGN

Thin, colored paper, about 8″ to 10″ square
Pencil
Scissors
White paper
White glue

1. Using a compass or a plate to trace around, draw a circle on the paper. Cut out the circle.

▶

Originally Polish *wycinanki* were cut using sheep shears. How such delicate, lacelike designs could be cut with such large scissors reveals how skilled the artisans were.

SAVE A TREE

Use recycled paper whenever you can. You can purchase pads of recycled note and drawing paper, but you can also make full use of *any* paper you use. Be sure to use both sides of each sheet of paper whenever possible, and turn scraps into note pads and tiny sketch books.

2. Fold the circle in half, colored-side facing in. Fold in half again, and in half once more. (A large circle cut from very thin paper can be folded in half yet another time.)

3. Draw a design on the paper, following the illustration or making up your own design. Remember that those portions that touch the edges are connecting points. The shaded parts in the illustration are the parts that get cut away.

4. Carefully cut out around the design. Open up the paper and glue it to a sheet of white paper. Frame the design by gluing the white paper to a slightly larger sheet of colored paper.

PICK A PACK OF PAPER

You're in for a surprise, when you discover what kinds of papers are available to artists. The nice thing is, much of the paper sold at art stores is sold by the sheet, so you can treat yourself to lots of different kinds.

For the cut-paper designs on this page, you can use origami paper, colored craft paper, even gift wrap (you'll find the greatest selection at card and party shops). Are you looking for a heavier paper that comes in colors? There's always construction paper, but another paper that comes in every color of the rainbow, and is not as brittle as construction paper, is a French paper known as Canson paper. It comes in 19″ × 25″ sheets, and is sold by the sheet.

Do you need an inexpensive paper that's just right for sketching on? Ask for newsprint pads. Tracing paper is another valuable paper with a lot of uses. It's available in different sized pads, as well as by the roll.

Watercolor papers are very heavy and can be used for constructing masks and models, as well as for painting on. Then there's poster board, which comes in a number of colors as well as white. Even heavier are the illustration and mat boards. Many art stores offer framing as one of their services, so you can usually buy small pieces of leftover mat board for very little.

And then there's colored tissue paper, foils, Japanese rice paper . . . the list goes on and on!

PRESSING MATTERS

Paper can be decorated in any number of ways, but embossing or decorating with a raised design is certainly one of the most subtle methods. Make your own note cards, bookmarks, or gift tags using this technique.

EMBOSSED NOTE CARDS

Small pieces of poster board
Scissors
X-acto knife
Heavyweight paper, such as watercolor paper
Boards, two 1″ × 6″ boards about 8″ long
Tape
Vise or 4 "C" clamps

Note A woodworker's vise or "C" clamps give the best results. If you don't have a vise or any clamps, use very heavy weights to give the necessary pressure.

1. Draw a simple design on a small piece of poster board. The design shown here is a cheerful sun, but choose anything that is meaningful to you. Cut the design out with the scissors; cut out any interior features with the X-acto knife.

2. Cut the heavyweight paper into pieces that will fit into envelopes when folded in half. (You can make the cards any size, if you also make your own envelopes. See page 26 for instructions.)

3. Place one of the boards on the work table. Position the cut-out cardboard face down in the center of the board, holding it in place with a piece of tape doubled over itself.

4. Dip the note-card paper in water to dampen it slightly. Place the paper over the cut-out. Put

the second board on top of this. Holding the boards firmly together (so the paper doesn't shift), place the boards in the vise and screw it closed as tight as you can. Let the paper dry, which should take about 8 hours.

5. Open up the vise and remove the paper. Fold the paper in half to make a note card.

Variations on a Theme
You can emboss paper with any number of objects. Form shapes out of wire or look for found objects such as metal washers, paper clips, or coins to impress onto paper.

Make an all-over design by sprinkling dried rice or beans on a flat surface that has first been coated with a waterproof glue such as rubber cement. Press in the usual way. Experiment with stretched-out plastic netting or knotted string laid down in an interesting pattern.

You'll get lasting results if you use thick paper and steady pressure. Experiment with different papers such as Canson paper, watercolor paper, and two-ply bristol board.

If you are using "C" clamps, screw one down in each corner of the board for the best results.

PRETTY IN INK

There are all sorts of inks available for both drawing purposes and for writing. There's no need to buy all the ink you use. Here's a recipe for a dist-ink-tive ink you can make yourself!

The Story of Art

The Chinese are thought to have discovered ink nearly 4,500 years ago. They made a black ink by mixing soot from burned oils with the resins and gums of various trees. This particular black is sometimes called lamp black, which refers to the earthenware lamps used to burn the oil.

Have you ever heard anyone say, "Just put your John Hancock right here"? What that person wants you to do is sign your name! John Hancock, whose signature was particularly handsome, was one of the signers of the Declaration of Independence.

BERRY INK
Sieve
Bowl
½ cup ripe berries (see *Note*)
½ teaspoon salt
½ teaspoon vinegar

Note Experiment with different berries. You can use blueberries, blackberries, raspberries, strawberries, elderberries, and cherries.

1. Place the sieve over the bowl. Push the berries through a sieve to extract all the juice. Throw the pulp and seeds away.

2. Add the salt and vinegar to the juice (and a tiny bit of water if the ink is too thick). Use a dip pen to either draw or write with the ink.

Store in a closed jar.

REED & QUILL PENS

Since you've made your own ink, why not make your own pens? Both reed and quill pens are easy to cut. Here's how:

Reed pens are made from hollow swamp reeds at least ¼-inch

WITH PEN IN HAND

There is a wide range of pens (brushes, too, see page 41 for more on these) that can be used with ink. Some nibs or points, such as the broader squared-off ones, are made especially for calligraphy, but you can use many nibs interchangeably. That's part of the fun—seeing what types of lines you can make with various pens.

Traditional pens are those that must be dipped often into the inkpot. They can be used with both waterproof and nonwaterproof inks. Be sure to clean your pens after use to prevent the dried ink from clogging the nibs.

Fountain pens, on the other hand, store ink in built-in holders. They are great for taking along when you do outdoor sketching. Some cannot be used with waterproof ink, so make sure you fill those with nonwaterproof inks only.

There are also pens known as reservoir pens that store ink. Technical pens belong in this category. These pens have points that make consistently wide lines. Draughtsmen (pronounced drafts-men) and illustrators use these quite often.

in diameter. (You can also use bamboo.) Gather your own reeds, if you like. If you pick them in late autumn, they are ready to cut; otherwise, let the reeds dry completely. With a very sharp knife (ask an adult to help you here), cut a piece about 8″ to 10″ long, and trim one end at an angle. Make a scoop-like cut on the underside.

Make a small slit in the middle of the tip.

Now shape the sides by trimming away just a little on either side of the slit. Leave the point sharp or cut it straight across.

Quill pens are made just the same way. The best quills are those from geese and turkeys. You may be able to find wild goose feathers on the ground or ask someone who raises barnyard fowl if you can take some fallen feathers.

Experiment with different angles and with different end-cuts. Reeds and quills that are cut short and stubby are best for drawing; those tapered to a long point are better for calligraphy. Quills, especially, need to be recut periodically as they wear down.

Goose quills were first used for writing around 1250.

INNER FEELINGS

The nicest greetings cards are the ones you make yourself. Here's a card that opens to reveal . . . something surprising!

POP-UP CARD

Medium-weight paper, 3 sheets about 8½″ × 11″
Crayons, markers, or paint
Scissors
White glue

Note You can make greeting cards any size you like, if you make your own envelopes (see *Signed, Sealed & Delivered* on page 26). If you'd rather use

ready-made envelopes, make your cards so that they fit comfortably in the envelopes when the cards are folded in half.

1. Cut two pieces of paper the same size. Fold each piece in half. In the middle of the folded side of one sheet of paper, cut two 1½″ slits about 2″ apart.

2. Fold the cut portion back; then straighten it out again. Open the paper and push this cut portion through to the other side.

Fold the paper in half again and open it up to test the pop-up portion.

▶

Christmas cards account for 60 percent of all greeting card sales. The average family sends 65 cards to friends and family each December.

There are many sizes and styles of envelopes, each known by a distinctive name. Baronial envelopes, for instance, are formal envelopes with a deep pointed flap. They are generally used for invitations and announcements. Policy envelopes are used to hold insurance policies, as well as various legal documents. Business envelopes, sometimes called officials, come in a number of sizes. No. 10 is the most popular size.

3. On another piece of paper, draw what you would like to pop up when the card is opened. Use the idea shown here, or come up with your own design. It shouldn't be much larger than the pop-up portion. Cut out what you have drawn and glue it to the card.

4. Glue the pop-up sheet you've just made to the other sheet of folded paper. Just squirt little drops of glue around the edges and in the middle. Make sure no glue is near the pop-up portion. Decorate both the front and the rest of the inside of the card.

Use just a little glue

Variations on a Theme
This is just one method of making a pop-up card. Another popular version is made by folding down the upper left-hand corner of the inner sheet to make a triangle.

Open the paper and push this triangle to the other side. Glue your pop-up figure to this inverted triangle, letting it extend above the card (it won't when the card is folded shut).

Use your imagination to add such touches as doors that open and figures that spring out (attach these to accordion-folded strips).

SIGNED, SEALED & DELIVERED

Envelopes come in all sorts of shapes and sizes, and you can make your own easily enough. Open up a purchased envelope to use as a pattern to trace around, or use the scaled-down patterns shown here.

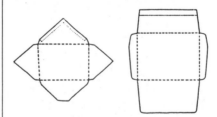

Choose a medium-weight paper that minimizes show-through but is light enough so that your card and envelope together weigh under an ounce (which is what a single first class stamp will cover).

Cut out as many envelopes as you need, fold them along the lines indicated, and glue all edges (except for the closing flap) with white glue or rubber cement. You won't be able to glue the flap down until you have the card in the envelope, but here's a trick you can use if you are making note cards with matching envelopes to give as gifts. Use mucilage (an amber-colored glue available at stationery stores) on the flap's edge, making sure you let it dry without sticking to anything. The glue can be licked later to close the envelope.

BOUND FOR GLORY

Binding books by hand is a real art. Here's a simple way to
make your own books, based on traditional Japanese bookbinding.
You're bound to be pleased with the results!

JAPANESE BOOKBINDING

Medium-weight paper, about 20 sheets, 8½" × 11"

Stiff paper for the cover (see *Note*)

Clothespins (optional)

Awl, ice pick, or hand drill

Embroidery thread or string

Large-eyed needle

Note Use embossed, printed, or marbled paper you have made yourself for the cover of your book. If your custom-designed paper isn't heavy enough, insert a piece of cardboard between the folds. Or glue the paper to cardboard as described in *Variations on a Theme*.

1. Fold the sheets of medium-weight paper in half lengthwise. Trim an inch or two off of each folded sheet to make the pages 5½" × 6½–7½" in size.

Traditional Japanese books are made with folded pages, but you can use single cut sheets if you prefer.

2. From the heavier paper, cut two covers for the book—one for the front, one for the back. Make them the same size as the pages. Use folded sheets for the cover, just as you did for the pages. (For some different ways of making covers, see *Variations on a Theme*.) Sandwich the pages between the covers.

3. On the front cover, mark a line of small dots along the spine's edge. These should be at least ½" from the spine, and anywhere from ½" to 1½" apart, depending on the size of your book and how you want it to look.

With the awl or some other sharp tool, poke holes through all the layers of the book. Clamp the pages of the book together with clothespins if you like. Insert the awl from the front, twisting it to make clean holes right through to the back.

4. Cut a piece of embroidery thread three times the length of the book, plus 12" or so extra. Thread the needle and sew the book together starting at the top.

▶

The Story of Art
Bookbinding, as we know it, had its start about the 4th century A.D. At first, flat or folded sheets of parchment were held together with leather thongs (laces). Eventually, a protective strip was placed over the book's spine, and hard covers were added to keep the pages flat and clean.

Paper folds best along the grain. How can you tell which way the grain runs? By folding a sample piece! A fold made along the grain is nice and crisp; against the grain, it's bumpy. The grain is less noticeable in handmade paper and in thin papers.

You can also tell which way the grain runs by tearing paper. Have you ever tried shredding a newspaper across its pages? For uniform strips, you must tear it from top to bottom. Which way do you think the grain runs in a newspaper?

The first public library was established in Rome around 39 B.C. The books housed there were all in scroll form.

Leave a few inches of thread dangling. Use a running stitch to get from the top of the book to the bottom.

Make the last stitch go around the bottom of the book and come back through that same last hole in the opposite direction.

Now work your way back up the spine, going around the spine at each hole, while also filling in the gaps left by the running stitch.

Tie the 2 loose ends of the thread together, making sure to go over the top of the book first. Pull the knot through the hole to hide it. Cut the thread.

Variations on a Theme

Experiment with different types of covers. Make a heftier one by pasting your cover paper to thin cardboard. Cut the cardboard the same size as your pages; cut the cover paper slightly larger on all four sides.

Cut the corners of the paper at an angle as shown. Paste the paper to the cardboard bringing up the sides and pasting them down firmly. Hide the raw edges with a smaller sheet of paper glued down.

Notice how the front cover is made in two pieces so that it will bend open more easily.

You can also make a rigid cover that has a cloth spine. Make a front and back cover (as described above) slightly larger than the book on all four sides. Cut a strip of tightly woven fabric, such as canvas, about 3½" wide by one-and-a-half times the book's length. Paste the covers to the spine.

canvas or other sturdy fabric

Make certain there is enough room between the front and back covers, so that the spine wraps around the book easily. Place the pages of the book inside the covers before making the holes for the binding thread.

There are many ways to bind books. Can you find any examples of books that are sewn? Check a hardbound book—most are sewn in signatures (groups) of 32 pages. How about books that are stapled? Or spiral-bound? Can you find an example of perfect binding, which is how many thick magazines are bound? Individual sheets are glued together at the spine. Another type of binding that looks almost the same but that holds up much better is known as Smythe-sewn binding. Signatures are first sewn and then glued to the spine. The book you are holding in your hand is Smythe-sewn.

SELF–CONTAINED

Here are two handy boxes that are perfect for holding small trinkets and treasures. The first box is folded from a single sheet of paper; the second is cut from cardboard and scored with a knife to make it easy to assemble.

FOLDED PAPER BOX

Medium-weight paper, 8½″ square
Scissors

Note The instructions here are for an open box measuring 3″ square by 1½″ deep.

1. Fold the paper diagonally in half, first one way and then the other. Unfold the paper.

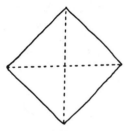

2. Fold all four corners so they meet at the center point. Unfold the paper.

3. Fold each corner to the crease lines made by the folds in step 2. Unfold the paper.

4. One by one, fold the corners so they meet the crease lines on the opposite side of the square, as indicated. Unfold the paper.

5. Your paper should look like this. Cut the paper along the thick lines indicated in the diagram.

6. Fold the sides down on the two opposite sides. Bend the sides in to form a box.

Fold the remaining two sides down so that the corner points meet in the middle.

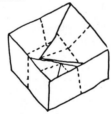

Variations on a Theme
Make a lid for your box by folding a square piece of paper that is 8¾″ in size, in exactly the same way.

You can turn your open box into a tiny basket by gluing a strip of paper over it as a handle.

Tricks of the Trade
Here's an easy way to make a square from a rectangular piece of paper. Make a diagonal fold in the paper, matching up one short side along one long side.

Cut away the extra bit at the one end and unfold.

▶

Poke holes in the top of this box to turn it into a dandy potpourri holder.

Paper that is too thin to score with an X-acto knife can be scored with a blunt tool such as a knitting needle.

CUT & SCORED CARDBOARD BOX

Sturdy cardboard, about 17″ × 21″
X-acto knife
Metal-edged ruler
White glue

Note The instructions here are for a cube-shaped box 5″ high. You can make yours any size by changing the dimensions of each side.

1. Draw the outline of a box on the piece of cardboard. Mark the folding lines with dotted lines, as shown in the diagram.

2. Cut the box out along the outlines. Score the folding lines by cutting through the cardboard only about halfway.

3. Glue the box together with a little white glue smeared on the tabs indicated. Do not glue the three flaps at the top. Decorate the outside of the box if you like.

Glue these tabs

Variations on a Theme
Boxes can be made in more shapes than just cubes. Make a box in the shape of a pyramid. Follow the diagram shown.

Or try something even more unusual. Here's the cutting pattern for a box that has 20 sides!

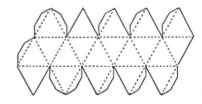

THE CUTTING EDGE

Scissors are fine for cutting most paper, but when you need to cut through thick cardboard or want to cut out interior sections, an X-acto knife works best. (X-acto is the brand name of one popular kind of craft knife, but the name is used loosely to mean any craft knife.)

X-acto knives come in several sizes, but a good choice is a holder that takes No. 11 blades. These blades are extremely sharp. Handle them with care or have an adult do the cutting for you.

Make sure you do your cutting on a surface that won't be ruined by the knife. Protect good countertops and tables with a large piece of cardboard placed under the items you're cutting.

To cut through thick cardboard, such as mat board, place a ruler (use a metal or metal-edged ruler because X-acto knives can accidentally nick wooden and plastic ones) on the line you want to cut and anchor it firmly with one hand. Draw the knife repeatedly along the ruler's edge, until you cut through the cardboard. It may take six or more slices before you cut through. If the line you are cutting is longer than the ruler, do one section at a time.

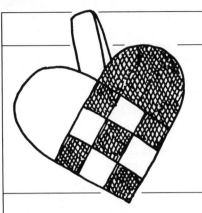

HEART TO HEART

Here's a heart-shaped basket that you may recognize as a traditional Swedish Christmas ornament. Don't save it for that time of year only. Make one anytime as a gesture of your affection.

WOVEN HEART BASKET

Medium-weight paper in 2 colors, each piece 3″ × 9″, plus a piece ½″ × 9″ (in either color)
Scissors
White glue

Note The instructions here are for a basket that measures approximately 4¼″ × 5″, not including the handle.

1. Fold each of the 3″ × 9″ rectangles in half crosswise, and round off the ends with the scissors.

2. Make two cuts in the folded end of each rectangle, 3″ long and 1″ apart.

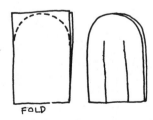

FOLD

3. Weave the basket by slipping the folded strips *around* and *through* each other, rather than over and under. Start by slipping the left-hand strip of the piece on your right around and through all three strips of the piece on your left.

Do the opposite with the second strip, slipping it through where you slipped the first one around, and so on. Do the last strip like the first.

Through   Around

4. Make a handle from the ½″ × 9″ piece of paper. Glue the ends to the inside of the basket.

Tip Change the woven pattern of the basket by varying the widths of the strips.

Make this heart basket out of felt. Secure the interwoven parts with glue to make the basket sturdier.

For more projects involving weaving, see *A-Tisket A-Tasket* on page 131, and *Handle with Care* on page 133.

FRAGILE
HANDLE WITH CARE

The heart is a universally understood symbol for friendship and love.

MARKING TIME

Often it's as much fun waiting for a special day to arrive as it is enjoying the day itself. Here's a special calendar that makes the most of the days preceding a birthday, holiday, or first day of summer!

The first fairly accurate measurement of a year's length was made by the Egyptians about 4200 B.C. Every year the Nile overflowed its banks at about the same time and that gave the Egyptians something to go by.

You may be familiar with Advent calendars. These traditionally have 24 windows and are meant to be opened from the first of December until Christmas Eve.

WINDOW CALENDAR

Medium-weight paper, 2 sheets about 14″ × 17″
X-acto knife
Colored pencils or markers
White glue

Note The instructions here are for a calendar that marks off 30 days. Make your calendar with as many openings as you like.

1. Place the two sheets of paper together on a firm surface. With a sharp pencil, draw the outlines of 30 windows on the top sheet of paper. (Make the window to be opened on the special day larger, if you like.) Press down on the pencil, so that the bottom sheet of paper has faint impressions of all the lines you draw on the top sheet.

2. Remove the top sheet and pencil in the window outlines on the bottom piece of paper. Draw little pictures in each space, coloring them in with colored pencils or fine-tipped markers. Make the drawings meaningful to you or the occasion.

3. Cut open the windows on the top sheet. Use the X-acto knife to cut three sides of each window

(the fourth side gets folded back when you open the window). Write the numbers 1 through 30 on the windows, scrambling the order. If you've made the last window larger and more important, make sure you number it 30. Decorate the top sheet in any way you like.

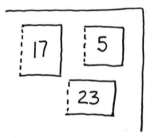

4. Carefully glue the top sheet to the bottom sheet. Make sure you don't put any glue too near any windows.

5. Hang the calendar. Thirty days before the special day, start opening the windows, one day at a time.

Tip Glue tiny beads to each window as handles, if you like.

LOOK SHARP

Colored pencils are perfect for detailed drawings such as the small pictures showing through the windows of this calendar. Of course, they can be used anytime you're working in color.

Colored pencils can be bought individually or in sets. Art stores usually carry several brands. Some have softer leads than others, and some are even water-soluble which means they can be used like watercolor paints.

You can get different effects with colored pencils by varying how hard you press down when you draw with them. Generally they work best when you press down lightly. You can blend two colors together to make a third (add more layers to create still more colors). You can also make new colors by placing one color over another in a cross-hatching pattern.

Notice that when you press down hard, you get deep, rich colors, but you can't blend them easily. Try a technique known as burnishing, instead. Make a drawing using light pressure on the pencils. Cover the entire drawing with a white (or other light color) pencil, pressing down hard to give the drawing a glazed finish. See how the colors get brighter but are slightly lighter. This occurs because white added to any color makes it a lighter shade.

PURE COLOR   COLOR + WHITE

Different countries use different calendars. The Chinese, for instance, not only number their years, but they also call them by name. Each year is named after one of twelve animals. They are, in order,

Year of the Rat
Year of the Ox
Year of the Tiger
Year of the Rabbit
Year of the Dragon
Year of the Snake
Year of the Horse
Year of the Sheep
Year of the Monkey
Year of the Rooster
Year of the Dog
Year of the Pig

The year 1990 is the Year of the Horse. Working your way backwards, you can find out what animal your birth year was named after. For example, if you were born in 1980, you were born during the Year of the Monkey. Do you share any of the characteristics of the animal of your year?

Most colored pencils are more difficult to erase than regular graphite pencils. (There is a brand that is erasable.) Correct any mistakes by gently scraping away the pencil marks with the blade of an X-acto knife.

FIRST IMPRESSIONS

The Chinese, who invented paper, also came up with an ingenious way to use it. They were the first to use paper for printmaking. The first printing blocks were probably the same stone carvings that had been used to make designs in clay wall tiles. The Chinese artists simply dabbed some paint on the carvings and pressed them down on paper. Printmaking was born!

LEAF IT BE

You needn't go far to find something to print with. Gather some fresh leaves from outdoors or from houseplants to make some eye-catching note cards.

LEAF–PRINT NOTE CARDS

Fresh leaves
Acrylic paints, in 1 or more colors
Brush
Scrap paper
Note cards or heavy paper cut to size

Note Acrylic paints are a good choice because the paint sticks to the waxy surface of most leaves.

1. If you aren't using purchased note cards, make your own from heavy paper folded in half. Just make sure the cards fit comfortably in standard-sized envelopes. (If they don't, make your own envelopes—see page 26.)

2. Choose fresh leaves that are whole and unblemished. (Fresh leaves work best, because they are pliable and the veins are more pronounced.) On the back of a leaf, brush on an even coat of paint.

3. Place the leaf, paint-side down, on the note card. Put a scrap of clean paper over the leaf and with your fingers (or a brayer or wooden spoon) rub the paper in the general area of the leaf.

2. Remove the paper and carefully peel back the leaf. Brush more paint onto the leaf to make more prints.

Tip You can easily change colors when you're using acrylics. These paints dry so quickly that you only need to wait a minute or so before brushing on a new color. You can also get some interesting effects by adding a new color before the old one is dry.

Variations on a Theme
Use this technique to print your own gift wrap and cover stock for the books you bind (see page 27). Dress up all sorts of household items with leaf prints. Use acrylic paints (the preferred paint because it is waterproof when dry) to decorate placemats, baskets, and planters.

Add a leaf-print border to a pair of curtains or to one of your T-shirts. Printed fabrics should be heat-set as described on page 37.

Don't stop once you've mastered leaf printing! Use your leaves to make leaf rubbings (place a leaf under a sheet of lightweight paper and rub over it with the flat side of a crayon) and leaf stencils (stick a leaf to a sheet of paper with a piece of tape doubled over itself, and dab paint around its perimeter). What other ways can you think of using leaves?

Leaves come in a variety of shapes. Most leaves are *simple,* with one leaf per stalk. Others are *compound,* with at least 3 (and as many as 36) leaflets attached to each stalk.

Leaves can be as long and skinny as evergreen needles (yes—they are leaves); they can be lobed, like maples and oaks, or shaped like small fans, such as the leaves of the ginkgo are.

Mix your own paints to match the colors of the leaves when they turn in autumn.

LOST & FOUND

Ever wonder what kind of print a potato masher makes? Now's your chance to find out. Here are two methods of printing that use items found in the home.

Try this for an interesting effect: Wrap some string around your brayer and roll the inked brayer directly on your paper.

FOUND OBJECT WRAPPING PAPER

Everyday objects such as bottle caps, string, kitchen utensils, shop tools, wood, and cardboard scraps
Printing ink (see *Note*)
Piece of glass, about 8½″ × 11″
Brayer
Large sheets of thin paper

Note For the best results, use water-based printing ink which is available at art stores.

1. Apply ink to the objects you are printing with in one of two ways. You can dip the items into a shallow dish containing slightly watered-down printing ink or paint. Or you can put some ink on a sheet of glass (you can also use a cookie pan), spread it out flat with a brayer, and roll the brayer over the objects you are printing with.

2. Press the inked objects down on the sheet of paper. Rock curved items back and forth slightly to make full contact with the paper.

3. See what kinds of designs you can make by combining various found objects.

See what kinds of patterns you can create with just one object.

Cover the entire paper with your design. Lay flat to dry.

Variations on a Theme
One-of-a-kind prints, known as monotypes, can be made in a slightly different way. Spread some printing ink on a sheet of glass with a brayer. Draw designs directly in the ink with various tools and found objects such as Popsicle sticks, forks, and cardboard scraps. You can even make a sampler of sorts by making a checkerboard pattern of different designs. Lay a sheet of paper over the glass and roll a clean brayer over it. Peel up the paper to reveal the print. Presto!

POTATO PRINT BOOKMARK

Potato
Paring knife
Printing ink
Piece of glass, about 8½″ × 11″
Brayer
Thick paper, about 2″ × 9″

1. Slice the potato in half. Make a simple raised design on the flat face of one half. Carve away those parts you don't want to print by slicing down and then across with the knife.

Let the potato dry for an hour or so to help the ink adhere better.

2. Spread some ink on the sheet of glass with the brayer. Dip the potato into the ink. Position the potato on the paper and press down firmly. Re-ink the potato after every one or two prints.

3. Use the potato to make a pattern that is evenly spaced, or place each print so that it is touching to create a different type of pattern.

POSITIVELY NEGATIVE

A funny thing happens when you print a repeated design with a potato, especially when the designs touch one another. The printed images make a pattern (this is the *positive* design), but so do the spaces between them (the *negative* design).

You can have a lot of fun playing around with patterns. Let some patterns just "happen," but experiment with using a grid to give others form. You can lightly pencil in grid lines to help you. Erase them when the ink is dry.

Here are a few grid patterns to try:

BLOCK

BRICK

DIAMOND

STRIPE

Look in your refrigerator for other vegetables and fruits to print with. Sliced green peppers, mushrooms, and broccoli and cauliflower flowerets make interesting prints. So do apples cut across the middle (see the star shape?) and citrus fruits sliced in half (let these dry for 2–5 days first).

Tricks of the Trade
Found objects and carved potatoes can also be used to print fabric. Use a water-based textile ink, and heat-set it to make it permanent and washable. Let the ink dry for 24 hours, then sandwich the fabric between clean paper towels and iron with a hot, dry iron for about 3 minutes. Keep the iron moving to avoid scorching the fabric.

RAISED CONSCIOUSNESS

Potatoes are perfect for printing small designs, but for larger images you'll want to use linoleum. Burlap-backed linoleum and the few tools used to cut it, aren't expensive. Ask for them at your local art store.

The Story of Art
Among the most beautiful woodcuts ever made are those that were made in Japan from about 1680 to the mid-1800s. At first black line prints were hand-colored with watercolors, but by 1764 full-color prints were made using inked blocks only. Ten and twelve different blocks were commonly cut for each print—one for every color.

Linoleum is harder to cut when it's cold. Warm it on a radiator (or in a 200°F oven) for a few minutes to soften it.

LINOCUT PRINTS
Linoleum, burlap-backed or mounted on wood blocks
Assorted cutting tools, plus a handle
Printing ink
Sheet of glass, about 8½″ × 11″
Brayer
Paper

Note Keep in mind that the image you make on the linoleum will print backwards. If you include any words in your design, make sure not only that they are spelled backwards, but that you form each letter in reverse. Check to see that you're doing it right by penciling the design on the linoleum (backwards) and hold it up to a mirror before cutting. It should read correctly.

1. Sketch your design on the linoleum with a pencil. Use the design shown here or make up your own.

Check that any letters are facing the right direction (see *Note*). Remember that mistakes cannot be corrected. You can always cut away more from a design to make it stand out from the background, but you can't replace any of the linoleum that you've already cut!

2. Hold the linoleum steady with one hand (watch that it is never in the way of the cutting tool). Hold the cutting tool in the other hand. Cut *away* from yourself. Turn the linoleum as needed, so that you're always cutting away from your body.

See *Gouge Gauge* on the next page for some of the effects you can get with just three blades.

3. Squeeze a little ink on the sheet of glass and spread it around with the brayer. When it is "tacky" (you can tell because it makes a smacking sound), roll the brayer over your linoleum block, covering it completely with ink.

4. Place a sheet of paper over the linoleum and apply even pressure with your hands or a clean brayer.

Or plunk the block down onto the paper. Push hard with your hands or even stand on the linoleum to make a complete impression.
Separate the linoleum and the paper, and leave the print to dry.

GOUGE GAUGE

You can achieve a variety of lines and textures with just three linoleum cutting blades. One handle can be used to hold the interchangable blades.

The knife-blade cutter is used to cut around shapes and to make thin lines. Two cuts are made with this tool for every line—one sloping away from the shape, the other right next to it, cut at the opposite angle. This makes a thin V-shaped line.

"V" tools also make V-shaped lines, but these come in a variety of widths. "V" tools are used to cut out sections of linoleum, especially where narrow but deep cuts are wanted.

Lastly, there are the U-shaped gouges, also available in several widths. These make a softer, wider line and are good for removing large areas, such as backgrounds.

For over 1,000 years, printing on paper was done solely with wood-cuts. Linocuts were introduced only with the invention of linoleum in the 19th century. Linoleum is much easier to cut than wood, but it lacks some of the crisp qualities inherent in wood.

STENCIL STATEMENTS

Stenciling is sort of a combination of printmaking and painting. The same image can be made over and over (as in printmaking), but a brush is used to dab on the paint (just like painting). Stencil your own stationery, or experiment with the effects you can create on fabric.

Use this trick to cut out stencils that are symmetrical or the same on both sides. Fold the thin cardboard in half before cutting and your time will be cut in half.

STENCILED STATIONERY

Tracing paper (optional)

Thin cardboard, about 4" × 6"

X-acto knife

Masking tape

Paint

Stiff-bristled brush

Typing paper, or plain stationery sheets

Note Tracing paper is handy when you are designing stencils. Use it to trace existing designs; use it also to help you position repeated designs on walls and furniture.

▶

40

The Story of Art
Stenciling probably originated in China. Some of the earliest examples we know of are paper patterns pricked with tiny holes that were used to stencil the outlines of paintings. It wasn't long before someone figured out that you could enlarge the open areas and stencil whole parts of the paintings themselves.

1. Draw the outline of your stencil on the thin cardboard. Draw it freehand, or trace an existing design and transfer it to the cardboard. (Sheets of clear acetate can also be used. Look for these wherever stenciling supplies are sold.) Use the design shown here, or make up your own.

2. Simplify your design to make it easier to "read." The outline of this apple, for instance, is made more interesting and easier to see by adding a vein to the leaf and by showing the contours of the apple with some white space.

This also allows you to stencil the apple in more than one color, if you choose. Make the apple red, the stem brown, and the leaf green, for example.

3. Carefully cut out the stencil shapes with the X-acto knife.

4. Tape the stencil in position at the top of a sheet of typing paper. With the brush, dab a little paint in the open areas, working from the edges toward the center (this keeps the paint from seeping under the stencil).

Use as little paint as possible (dab the excess off onto scrap paper first). Use a different brush for each color.

5. Let the paint dry before removing the stencil. Tape it to the next sheet of paper, and stencil it. Continue in this way until you are done.

MULTICOLORED STENCILED T-SHIRT
Tracing paper
Thin cardboard, 3 pieces about 8″ × 10″
X-acto knife
Masking tape
Water-based textile paints or acrylics, in 3 colors
Stiff-bristled brush
Newspaper
T-shirt

Note This stenciled design is meant to be made in three colors, one at a time. Separate stencils are cut for each color.

1. Draw the outline of your design on a piece of tracing paper. Use the design shown here or make up your own. Lightly pencil a box around the drawing and mark each corner of the box with a dot.

2. Transfer the outline of the earth (make a 7″ circle using a plate or compass) to one of the pieces of thin cardboard. Transfer the dots marked in the four corners, too.

Transfer the outlines of the continents to a second piece of cardboard. Transfer the dots marked in the four corners.

Lastly, transfer the word "HOME" to the last piece of cardboard. Transfer the corner dots.

3. Carefully cut out the stencil shapes on each piece of cardboard. Poke small holes in each where the dots are.

4. Lay the T-shirt on a flat surface. Fold up some newspaper and place it between the front and back of the shirt. Smooth out any wrinkles and bumps.

5. Position the first stencil on the shirt. Tape it down. Poke a sharp pencil or water-soluble fine-tipped marker through the holes in the four corners. (Make sure the dots show up on the shirt.)

6. Paint the open area of the stencil, in this case using a bright blue. Work from the edges toward the center. Use as little paint as possible, dabbing it on with an up-and-down motion. Let the paint dry; then remove the stencil.

7. Position the second stencil on the shirt, matching up the marks in the four corners. Tape the stencil down. Paint the open areas, in this case, green, adding more paint in some areas to suggest shading. Let dry and remove the stencil.

Do the same with the third and last stencil.

8. Let the shirt dry 24 hours. Remove the newspaper and replace it with clean paper towels. Put a few sheets of paper towels over the design. Iron the shirt for at least 3 minutes with a hot, dry iron. Keep the iron moving all the time to prevent scorching. This heat-setting makes the shirt washable.

Keep delicate parts of stencils flat by pressing them down with a pencil held in your free hand.

BRUSHING UP

Artists' brushes fall into two main categories: those made from soft hair such as squirrel hair, red sable, or synthetic hair, and those stiffer-bristled brushes made from hog hair or synthetic fibers.

The softer brushes are generally used for painting with watercolors and for very detailed work. Pointed brushes, especially, are used for precise work. Large, flat brushes known as one-stroke brushes are perfect for laying down broad expanses of color.

Bristle brushes are better suited to oil and acrylic painting. They come in a variety of shapes and sizes. Stencil brushes are stubby, round brushes made from bristles, although you can stencil with any stiff-bristled brush.

A good brush will last a very long time, if you treat it with care. Avoid getting paint on the ferrule or metal part of the brush that holds the hairs in place. The paint will gradually weaken the hair at that point and the brush will start shedding. Always clean your brushes as soon as you are done using them. Store brushes in a jar, bristle-end up, to keep the hairs nice and straight.

Stenciling was commonly used to decorate walls (and sometimes floors) in colonial America. Wallpaper was expensive and hard to come by. Traveling artists called limners went from town to town stenciling designs and painting murals on walls in homes and public buildings.

Drawing with brush and ink is highly developed in China. Brush drawing as an art form first appeared in the West in the 15th century.

SCREEN STARS

Screen printing is basically a stencil technique using a frame that has finely-woven mesh stretched over it. You can print with one, two, or more colors. Here's how to work two colors into a print.

The Story of Art

The mesh used in screen printing was originally made of silk, and the method was commonly called silkscreen printing. Silkscreen printing was used long ago to print textiles, but it wasn't until the beginning of this century that screen printing was used to make art prints.

TWO-COLOR SCREEN PRINT
Tracing paper, 2 sheets 8½″ × 11″
Medium-weight paper, 8½″ × 11″
X-acto knife
Masking tape
Screen printing ink in 2 colors
Hinged screen and squeegee (see page 43)

1. On an 8½″ × 11″ piece of paper, draw a picture or design to be printed in two colors. Use the picture shown here, or draw one of your own. Keep the shapes simple and bold.

2. Place a sheet of tracing paper directly over the drawing (have all the edges matching), and trace around those parts that are going to be printed in the lightest color. The sky and part of the water in this picture, for instance, are pale blue.

Carefully cut out these sections with the X-acto knife.

3. Do the same for the parts of your drawing that are going to be printed in the second color. In this case, the flag, the stripes on the sail, and the rest of the water are a blue-green. Make sure you place this tracing paper directly over the drawing as you did with the first piece, so that the two stencils line up properly when you put one on top of the other.

4. Place a large sheet of scrap paper on the board under the screen. Put the first stencil on top of the paper, making sure it sits exactly under the screen when it is lowered. Pour some ink at the end of the screen farthest from you. Pull the squeegee towards you, dragging the ink along. Lift the screen; the stencil is now stuck to it.

↓ Bring squeegee forward

5. Place an 8½″ × 11″ piece of paper on the board under the screen. Try to position it right under the screen so that the printed image will not be crooked. Place some masking tape on the board at all four corners of the paper. Lower the screen, ink it, and make a print. Lift the screen and check to see that the print is where you want it on the paper.

Make any necessary adjustments, moving the masking tape accordingly.

6. Make as many prints as you like, one after another, positioning the paper within the masking tape lines each time. Set the prints aside to dry.

7. Remove the stencil and wash the screen with warm, soapy water. (Wash the squeegee if you're using the plastic kind.) Let dry. Place the second stencil on the board beneath the screen; carefully position it between the masking tape. Adhere the stencil to the screen, as you did the first one.

8. Place one of the already-printed papers on the board between the masking tape lines. Lower the screen; print with the second color. Remove the paper and set aside to dry. Continue printing until you have added the second color to all the sheets. Wash the screen and squeegee.

SCREEN & SQUEEGEE

You can make your own screen printing set-up very easily with some wood, hardware, and finely-woven fabric. (You can also buy small screens and squeegees at most art stores.)

A screen with inside dimensions of 8½" × 11" is a good size to start out with. Have a lumber-yard rip some 1" × 3" pine boarding down the middle. Cut four pieces and attach them at right angles with corner braces or irons.

Staple some polyester mesh to one side of the frame (ask for this at an art store, or pick up some organdy or tightly-woven curtain material at a fabric store). Cut the mesh at least 4" larger than the frame all around, and stretch it as tightly as possible as you staple it to all four sides.

To prevent the mesh from ripping, you can place a strip of thin cardboard over it before stapling. Trim away the excess mesh.

Run masking tape along the inside of the frame to keep the ink from seeping under the screen.

Cut a piece of masonite or ¼" plywood 2" larger than the frame. Bolt a piece of wood to one end of the masonite (have the nuts at the top). Place the screen (screen-side down) against the bolted wood piece. Join them together with two hinges. Screw an "arm" to one side of the screen, so you can prop the screen up.

And what about a squeegee? You can easily make your own from a scrap of thick cardboard about 4" × 8", or you can buy the thick plastic kind at an art store.

Tricks of the Trade
There are a number of different ways of creating a stencil for screen printing. You can draw directly on the screen with lithographic tusche or crayons (just remember that what you draw on the screen will not print, but will be the color of the paper). You need to use water-based ink when you use this method (so that the ink won't dissolve the stencil), but you'll need turpentine to clean away the design.

You can also use stencil film that is coated so that it sticks to the screen when wet (some films are water-based, others shellac-based). Check to see what your art store stocks.

ANYTHING GOES

Some art tells a story; some is a record of people and places. Abstract art is art that has no "subject."

Abstract art is appreciated for its color and form, and, in the case of collages, for its texture. There may be no recognizable objects in abstract art, but it can be very expressive.

SPONGE & SPATTER

Sponge painting is a quick way to give a textured look to walls, furniture, and pottery. Use this method to make a colorful planter for yourself or as a gift for a gardening friend.

SPONGE–PAINTED PLANTER

Flower pot, terracotta or plastic
Sponge
Scissors or X-acto knife (optional)
Acrylic paint

1. Wash and dry the flower pot.

2. Tear or cut the sponge into small pieces about 2″ square. You can also cut the sponge into shapes such as circles, triangles, stars, or letters of the alphabet. Use the X-acto knife to cut out interior sections.

3. Squeeze acrylic paint on some newspaper and dip the sponge into it. Press the sponge on the flower pot, in a random pattern, or, in the case of letters and other shapes, with some space between each print.

Experiment with sponging a different color over the first one, or even a third color. Let the paint dry completely.

Variations on a Theme
Spatter painting is another decorating technique that's fun to do. You need an old toothbrush (or a paintbrush), a Popsicle stick, and some watery paint.

Spatter painting can be very messy! Be sure to use only water-based paints and protect both yourself and your work area from flying paint. For small pieces, do your spattering in a cardboard box. Otherwise, work outdoors if possible. Water-based paints will not harm grass or other plants.

Dip just the tip of the brush's bristles in the paint. Hold the brush over the surface you are decorating and draw the Popsicle stick across the bristles. Bring the stick *towards* you; otherwise you'll end up spattering yourself! Keep moving the brush to spread the spatters around. Repeat with different colors.

Comb painting is another decorating technique. Make a "comb" from a scrap of sturdy cardboard. (You can also buy combs made of flexible rubber or metal notched with teeth of various widths.) Cut a row of notches in the cardboard with a pair of scissors or an X-acto knife.

Dip the comb in some paint and pull it across the surface you are decorating. Experiment with making choppy and wavy lines, full circles and woven patterns.

Artist's Profile
One well-known painter made his mark with spattered paint. Jackson Pollack, an American painter who lived from 1912 to 1956, created many huge canvases of dripped and spattered paint. He often lay the canvas on the floor of his studio and stood over it flinging paint. Sometimes, he squeezed paint right from the tube onto the canvas or punctured holes in paint cans and swung them about. This style of painting came to be known as *action painting*.

STONE CLONE

Marbling is a popular way of decorating paper used in bookbinding and desk accessories. Use your marbled paper to cover a notebook or to make a pencil holder from an empty oatmeal box.

Marbling was once a carefully controlled craft. Apprentices were taught only part of the process, so that they couldn't make marbled paper on their own.

OIL & WATER MARBLED PAPER

Medium-weight paper
Oil paints, 2 or 3 colors
Turpentine or mineral spirits
Paper cups
Plastic dishpan or deep tray
Paint brush
Small stick
Notebook
Rubber cement

Note Make sure the paper fits comfortably in the dishpan or deep tray you are using. Trim the paper if necessary.

1. Thin each oil paint color with a little turpentine in the paper cups. The paint should be thin enough to shake easily from a brush. (It shouldn't be too runny or it will spread out to nothing when it is dropped on the water.)

2. Fill the dishpan with room-temperature (65–70°F) water at least 3″ deep. With the paint brush, sprinkle small drops of each color onto the water. Use a small stick, such as a toothpick, to make swirling designs in the water. Don't overmix, or the colors will get muddy.

3. Hold the paper by opposite corners and carefully lower it onto the water. Let it lie flat, then lift it out of the water. Dry the paper flat, design-side up, on newspaper or hang to dry.

4. Glue the paper to the cover of a notebook such as a spiral-bound pad. Trim any excess off.

Tip Use the same tray of water to make more marbled designs. Simply add more drops of color to the dishpan. Or start fresh by skimming any remaining paint from the water with a strip of newspaper. Drop new paint on the water.

Marbled paper made with only one color is also effective, especially when done with colored paper.

▶

WALLPAPER PASTE MARBLED PAPER

Medium-weight paper
Powdered wallpaper paste
Oil paints, 2 or 3 colors
Turpentine or mineral spirits
Plastic dishpan or deep tray
Paint brush
Small stick
Oatmeal box
Rubber cement
Scissors

1. In a medium-sized bowl, mix ¾ cup of wallpaper paste with 4 cups of room-temperature (65–70°F) water. Stir until well blended. Add another cup of water to make the paste thick and sauce-like. Pour the paste into the dishpan.

2. Mix your oil paints with turpentine as described in step 1 of *Oil & Water Marbled Paper.* Drop the colors onto the paste in an all-over design. With the stick, move the colors around in swirling, zig-zagging, or scalloped patterns.

3. Hold the paper by opposite corners and lower it onto the paste. Lift the paper out of the dishpan and sponge the paste off the paper under running water. Be careful not to rub the marbled pattern off. Dry the paper flat, design-side up, on newspaper or hang to dry.

4. Cut the paper so that it is about an inch wider than the oatmeal box you are covering and 1″ to 2″ longer. Glue the paper to the box with rubber cement. Position it so there is paper overhanging at both the top and bottom of the box.

5. Turn the excess paper at the top to the inside of the box and glue it down.

6. Cut notches out of the excess paper at the bottom, and glue the paper to the bottom of the box. Cut a circle of paper slightly smaller than the bottom of the box and glue it to the bottom.

Use marbled paper to cover the books you bind (see page 27). A woven heart basket made from marbled paper is nice (see page 31). So, too, are boxes (page 29) and rolled paper beads (page 152).

The Story of Art
The Japanese were marbling paper as early as the 8th century, but the technique was not widely used until the Persians and Turks took up the craft in the 1500s.

Examples of marbling made their way to western Europe from the Middle East. Bookbinders began using larger sheets of marbled paper as end papers. In the 17th century in England, there was a high tariff or tax on imported papers. To get around this, some merchants used marbled paper to wrap small items that were being shipped to England. As the paper was simply "packing material," it escaped being taxed. When the crates were unpacked, the sheets of marbled paper were smoothed out and sold to the bookbinders!

DIP DESIGNS

Tie-dyeing is a popular way to decorate fabric (see page 143), but you can use a similar method to color paper. This paper is pretty enough to frame, but you can also use it to wrap gifts or make covers for books.

This method of decorating paper is very popular in Japan where it is called *itajime-shibori.* Soft folded-and-dyed paper is sometimes used as napkins for special occasions.

FOLD–AND–DYE WRAPPING PAPER

Absorbent paper, such as paper napkins and towels or rice paper

Assorted colored inks or food colors

Note This project goes fast. Practice with inexpensive paper, such as paper towels, before using rice paper.

1. Pour the ink into small dishes. (Two or three different colors is plenty.) Thin the inks with a little water.

2. Fold a paper towel in half width-wise, and in half again.

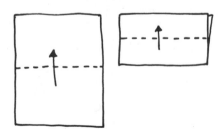

3. Fold the top left-hand corner down to the bottom edge.

Then fold this triangular section to the back.

Continue folding back and forth in this way, making a series of folded triangles.

4. Compress the paper with your fingers and dip each corner of the triangle into the ink. Hold the

paper in the ink for only a second or two—the paper quickly soaks up the dye.

5. Carefully unfold the paper and hang to dry.

Variations on a Theme
Experiment with other ways of folding the paper before dipping it in the ink. Fold the paper into a narrow strip (as you did for the triangular folds above), but fold it into squares instead.

Try this variation, too. Fold the paper first one way and dye it. Let it dry and then fold it another way and over-dye it.

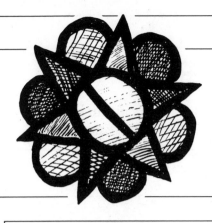

WINSOME WINDOWS

Colored glass windows rely on sunlight to bring them to life. The jewel-like colors can be really dazzling. Transform one of your windows into a "stained glass" window with this tissue paper technique.

PAPER "STAINED GLASS" DESIGN

Heavy-weight black paper, about 20″ × 30″
Tissue paper in assorted colors
X-acto knife
White glue

1. On a separate piece of paper, draw a geometric design. Use the design shown here or make one of your own.

Make the lines of your drawing at least ½″ wide. The tissue paper will be glued to the back of these lines, so they must be wide enough.

2. Transfer the design to the sheet of black paper. Carefully cut out all the open spaces with an X-acto knife.

AT LEAST ½″ WIDE

3. Choose what color tissue paper you want for each cut out section. Do one section at a time. Cut the tissue paper roughly to size. Spread a little glue on the back of the black paper that frames that section. Place the tissue paper over the opening and press it all around. Trim off any excess tissue paper.

Continue to cover each opening with tissue paper. Let dry.

4. Hang the "stained glass" design in a sunny window, glued-side against the pane.

The art of stained glass reached its peak in the 13th century. By the 1600s, the art was nearly forgotten. It was revived in the 1800s when windows modeled on medieval examples were made once again. It wasn't long before original designs in stained glass became popular.

Tricks of the Trade
To transfer a design, rub pencil on the back of the design. Place the design pencil-side down on a second sheet of paper. Carefully trace all the lines of the design; lift the paper. The design is now on the second sheet of paper.

Originally, stained glass windows were used as instructional aids in churches and chapels. Scenes from the Bible or from the lives of the saints were illustrated for all to see in this way.

BITS & PIECES

Collages are wonderful catch-all pieces of art. You can make them with everything from sticks and stones to postage stamps and pictures cut out of magazines. Here's a collage that pays tribute to where you live.

Collages were "invented" by Pablo Picasso, a Spanish painter who created some very original art during his 92-year lifetime. Pasting items on boards is an old folk art, but Picasso is credited with turning collages into fine art.

Another name given to collages is *assemblage* —artwork made of many things assembled together.

NEIGHBORHOOD COLLAGE

Things you find in your neighborhood, from rubbings of tree bark and manhole covers to your local newspaper and candy wrappers
Sturdy cardboard (see *Note*)
X-acto knife
White glue or hot glue

Note Cardboard is fine for gluing paper and lightweight objects to. Use a heavier support, such as 1/4″ plywood or masonite, for bulkier items. Likewise, white glue works well with paper, but hot glue is a better choice for heavier items.

1. Collect items for your collage. Make rubbings of tree leaves, as well as engraved signs and building bricks. Look for things that have meaning for you—movie ticket stubs, bags from local merchants, pictures of your favorite cartoon characters.

2. Make a "frame" for your collage. (A purchased frame with glass can be used for flat collages.) Cut 1″-wide strips of cardboard and glue them around the perimeter of the cardboard you are using for the collage. This gives the collage a finished look.

3. Play around with the arrangement of your collected items. Large flat pieces can form the background for smaller things; related items might look good grouped together. When you are happy with the way everything looks, glue the pieces down.

The word collage is from the French word *coller* which means "to glue."

Variations on a Theme
Here are some other ideas for collages.

Make a nature collage. Paste down twigs, leaves, pieces of bark, feathers, moss, rubbings of rocks . . . you name it.

Make a collage with items all the same color. If there's something you want to add to your collage, but it's the wrong shade, then paint it.

Make a collage with things you've saved from a vacation trip.

This is a great way to keep those memories alive.

STICK TO IT

There are many glues available to artists, some better suited to certain materials than others. The two most often suggested in this are white glue and rubber cement.

White glue, such as an all-purpose glue like Elmer's® glue, is perfect for porous materials such as paper, wood and fabric. Because it is a watery glue, it has a tendency to bleed through thin materials and buckle others. Use white glue very sparingly, and spread it out with your fingers to get more coverage. It can also be thinned with water and brushed on. Clean your brushes and hands with warm, soapy water.

Rubber cement is also used for gluing paper. There are two types: regular rubber cement that is brushed on both surfaces and allowed to dry before bonding, and the type known as one-coat rubber cement, which requires—you guessed it—coating just one surface. Regular rubber cement is more widely available, and is the one called for in this book.

After sticking your paper down with rubber cement, burnish (rub hard) the paper to create a good bond. Clean any excess from your artwork by rubbing it off with your fingers. Rubber cement peels away very easily. If you accidentally glue the wrong paper down, or glue it on crookedly, carefully peel the top paper off, clean the rubber cement from both surfaces and start again. Rubber cement can be thinned with rubber cement thinner if it begins to evaporate and thicken. (See *Safety Check* on page 11 for proper storage and use of rubber cement.)

Wood glue, a water-based glue used for gluing wood to wood, is useful when making collages. Wood glue (as well as such glues as epoxy and super adhesives) can be purchased at hardware and department stores.

Most glues are derived from animal substances, such as bones and skin.

RUB DOWN

Abstract art makes the most of color and form . . . and texture. What better way to show texture than to make a rubbing? Look for rough, bumpy surfaces and those with raised patterns.

ABSTRACT RUBBING

Anything with texture, from tree bark to coins

Soft pencils or crayons

Thin paper, about 8½″ × 11″

Note Thin paper works best for making rubbings. There's a large selection to chose from. Try out such papers as tracing paper, thin typing paper, and many of the Oriental papers.

1. Make an abstract picture of randomly placed rubbings. Place your paper over whatever you are rubbing. With your fingers, feel where the object is located. Use a soft pencil or a crayon to make back-and-forth strokes over the

▶

Texture is all around us. Close your eyes and rub your hands along some textured items. Can you tell what they are without looking?

object. Use light pressure for the best results.

Variations on a Theme
Compose a picture made up of textures taken from various objects. A landscape can be made with different textures for fields, mountains, and clouds. Draw a portrait of a person and "clothe" him with shirt and pants made by rubbing over textured surfaces.

Many people enjoy making rubbings of old gravestones. Some of the old grave markers are decorated with quaint carvings.

COLOR CODED

Can you imagine what it would be like if everything were in black and white? Color plays an important part in everyday life. You probably respond to some colors more favorably than others. Look how some colors "respond" to one another!

We use color names in many common expressions. When someone is sad, we say he's blue; an angry person is said "to see red." If you're green with envy, you're jealous. What other expressions can you think of?

COLOR STUDIES
Paint, markers, or crayons, in assorted colors
Brush, for paint
Masking tape (optional)
Paper or canvas

Note You can also use cut paper for these color studies. Check your scrap box for pieces of paper in solid colors.

1. Create a series of paintings concentrating on color combinations. Start out with using just two colors. Cover the paper completely with one color; let it dry. Paint a square or other shape in the center of the paper, using the other color.

Do a series of these paintings, keeping the background color constant while changing the color of the central shape.

Notice how the background color looks different depending on the color next to it.

2. Evoke different moods with your color studies. How would you show "quiet" or "hot"? Use the brushstrokes (or marker and crayon lines) to help you express these moods.

3. Make some paintings using as many colors as you like. Which colors seem to work well together? Experiment with little paintings, and very large ones (tape together several sheets of large paper to create mural-size compositions).

ROUND & ROUND

Color and its effects have been closely studied by artists over the centuries. You may be familiar with the basic color wheel, a tool which can help you understand the relationship between colors. You can make your own color wheel using the model shown here. Fill in the "pie slices" with colored markers or crayons.

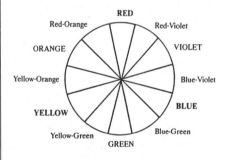

The colors in **bold type** are the *primary colors.* Mix them together to create the *secondary*

colors (red + blue = violet, blue + yellow = green, yellow + red = orange). *Intermediate colors* are created whenever you mix a primary color with a secondary color (red + violet = red-violet, for instance).

The colors opposite one another on the wheel are known as *complementary colors* (red and green are complementary, for example). These are exciting colors when used together.

You can make any color lighter by adding white (the new color is called a *tint*). You can make any color darker by adding a little black (these are called *shades*).

Experiment with isolating colors with black or white strips (such as you did with the paper "stained glass" design on page 49). Placed next to black, colors seem to glow; next to white, they appear darker.

In commercial printing, full-color printing is done using three different primary colors. These are yellow, magenta (a bright purpled-red) and cyan (a turquoise blue). Inks in these three colors plus black are combined to create the thousands of colors the human eye is able to distinguish.

Most animals see in black and white (and shades of gray). Monkeys, apes, many birds, and some fish, however, apparently have vision similar to ours. Bees are another exception, but experiments show they are not able to distinguish the color red.

THE ARTFUL ANIMAL

Some of the earliest art we know of was created nearly 20,000 years ago on the walls and ceilings of caves. What do you suppose those artists chose to paint? You guessed it—animals! Artists continue to try to capture the beauty, majesty, and mystery of animals in their art. But not all the animals people paint and sculpt are real. Just think of the fabulous dragons that the Chinese make or the frightening animal masks that are found in so many cultures.

PET PROJECT

There's something about animals that makes us want to touch them. Make a portrait of your pet, if you have one, or of an animal you admire, that shows how soft its fur is or how slithery its skin!

ANIMAL COLLAGE

| Scraps of felt and fake fur, yarn, cotton balls, sandpaper, art papers |
| Dried peas and beans, spices, beads, sequins |
| Paint or markers |
| Poster board, about 8½" × 11" |
| White glue |

1. Draw the outline of an animal (or of several) on the piece of poster board. Place your animal in an outdoor setting, the way these sheep and cows are, or wherever you like.

2. Fill in the outlines with your chosen materials. Use white glue to hold them in place. The sheep here are made with cotton balls and black turtle beans (for the face and feet); the cows' spots are made from sandpaper cut into shapes.

Experiment with fake fur (perfect for cuddly creatures) and short pieces of yarn for manes and tails. Use overlapping sequins to create a spangled snake; crumple up some grey paper, smooth it out, and glue it down for an elephant's hide. Use shiny paper or cellophane to make a fish.

QUICK TAKES

There are other ways of making a portrait of your pet, of course. Sleeping pets, especially, are cooperative models. Spend some time making pencil sketches of the different poses your pet sleeps in.

Here's something a little different. Try "suggesting" your pet's shape with as few lines as possible. This is harder than it looks! For bolder lines, use a crayon or brush and ink. With just a few lines you can get the feeling of a solid form.

The Story of Art
The beautiful paintings of animals on cave walls and ceilings were not meant to be seen and admired. Instead, they were created for their magical powers. How do we know this? Since many primitive tribes living today use art in a similar way, we can guess that when a cave artist painted a picture of a bison, he was casting a sort of spell over a real bison. After all, our ancestors depended on animals for food and clothing, and they did what they could to make sure they had enough.

LIONS & TIGERS & BEARS

The Huichol (WEE-chole) Indians of Mexico make decorative paintings of animals using brightly-colored yarn. They press the yarn into soft beeswax spread on a board, but you can use white glue for the same effect.

Yarn and beeswax paintings are traditionally made by the Huichol men. The women make a similar type of art by pressing tiny glass beads into wax that is shaped into small animal sculptures.

The art of spinning wool into yarn was developed around 4000 BC.

YARN PAINTING
Stiff cardboard, about 6″ square
Yarn in assorted colors
White glue
Scissors

Note Yarn paintings can be any size, but because they take time to make, it's best to start small.

1. Draw the outline of an animal on the cardboard. (Most Huichol yarn paintings have a single figure, filled in with several colors of yarn.) Make the cat as shown here or draw your own animal. If there are distinct areas that you are going to fill with different colors, sketch in those lines, too.

2. Start by covering the outlines with yarn. Spread some glue in the general area, then press the yarn down, following the outline all the way around. Cut the yarn when you reach the spot where you began.

3. Fill in the figure with yarn, working from the outside in. Spread the glue in small areas and press the yarn in place, keeping the strands as close to one another as possible. The painting will have a swirling pattern. Change colors by cutting the yarn of the first color and placing the start of the second color right after it.

4. Now fill in the background. Start by making a border around the whole piece with one or more colors of yarn. Then work the background in a solid color. Again, start at the outer edge and work in. When one area gets completely filled in, cut the yarn and fill in another area.

Tip Try not to press too hard on the yarn when you are gluing it in place. It will stay nice and clean, and springy, too, if you handle it gently.

The Spanish explorers brought sheep to the New World in the early 1500s.

MYTHICAL MONSTERS

The dragon is one make-believe monster common to countries in both the West and the East. With this painting technique, you can give your fire-breathing dragon a smoky smile!

BLEACH PAINTING

Heavyweight paper, about 8½" × 11"
Fountain pen ink (see *Note*)
Brush
Bleach
Popsicle stick

Note Some fountain pen inks work better than others for this project. Skrip® ink is recommended for the best results. Use black or a blue-black for a picture that really stands out.

1. Cover the entire sheet of paper with the ink. Swirl the ink around to make a murky background. Set aside to dry.

2. With the Popsicle stick, paint a picture of a dragon (or the beast of your choice) using the bleach. The dragon will magically appear as the liquid bleaches the ink. Make plenty of smoke coming out of the dragon's nostrils with swirling lines.

Variations on a Theme
Let the bleach completely dry. Then add color to the painting with markers, pastels, or crayons.

Add color to bleached areas

Be very careful handling the bleach. Do this project in a well-ventilated area and protect both your work area and yourself from splashes. A single drop of bleach will make a permanent white spot, if it falls on colored fabric.

FADE AWAY

Usually when you draw or paint, you *add* color to white paper to make an image. With bleach painting, however, you start with a colored background and bleach out those parts you want to show up. Bleach paintings are very dramatic because the reversed image (white on black or some other dark color) really stands out.

Bleach painting can also be done with dyed fabrics. Dark colors work best here, too. Use chlorine bleach (rather than the type of bleach which doesn't affect dyes) to paint a design on the fabric or to dip a tightly-wadded up ball of fabric into. (This technique is a type of tie-dyeing. For more projects using this method, see *Dip Designs* on page 48, and *To a Tee* on page 143.)

Chinese people all over the world celebrate their New Year (which falls some time in mid-February) with firecrackers and a huge dragon that dances in the streets. The dragon is actually an enormous costume that is worn by as many as 50 people!

FLYING FISH

The Japanese are famous for their kites, but they also make a wind sock in the shape of a carp, a favorite fish. It is displayed each year on May 5th during the festival once known as Boys' Day, but now more appropriately called Children's Day.

The carp is a fish that swims upstream against the current. To the Japanese, the fish is a symbol of strength, courage, and determination, all qualities they want their children to have.

For a kite you can make that really flies, see page 88.

FABRIC WIND SOCK

White fabric, about 16″ × 24″
Acrylic paints
Brush
Plastic lid from a coffee can
Scissors
Needle and thread
String

Note You can also make this wind sock out of paper (in which case, glue the seams rather than sew them). It won't hold up very long if hung outdoors, but it's just as nice.

1. Fold the fabric in half lengthwise and draw the outline of a fish on it. Place the bottom of the fish on the fold of the fabric. Make sure the fish's mouth measures 4½″, so that it will fit snugly around the coffee can lid when it's sewn. Cut along the outline.

2. Open up the fabric, and place it on some newspaper. Paint the fish with acrylic paints so that both sides match. Let the paint dry.

3. Poke a hole in the center of the coffee can lid with the scissors and cut out the entire center, leaving just the rim.

4. Fold the fish along the center fold, right sides together, and stitch the long edge with small, even stitches. Place the lid rim around the fish's mouth and fold about an inch of fabric over the rim, concealing it. Stitch the fabric in place.

Fold fabric over rim and stitch

5. Turn the fish right side out. Cut a piece of string about 20″ long. Poke two small holes in the fabric on opposite sides of the mouth and tie the string to the rim. Tie another, longer string to the middle of the first one. Lash the wind sock to a pole or porch railing, so it is blown horizontally when there's a breeze.

TUMBLEBUGS

Bet you've never seen an insect flip-flop quite like this one! Don't tell your friends what makes this little critter go, and see if they can guess.

TUMBLING TOY

Poster board, about 4″ × 8″
Scissors
White glue
Marble
Paint or markers
Felt or paper scraps

1. Cut a ¾″ × 4½″ strip and two ovals, ¾″ × 1¾″, from the poster board.

2. Glue the long strip into an oval shape, overlapping the ends about ¼″. Hold the ends together until the glue sets. Glue one of the poster board ovals to one edge of the strip. Let dry.

3. Place the marble in the tumbler and glue the other oval in place. Let dry. Turn the tumbler into a tumblebug by adding a little paint, six felt feet, and a pair of antennae.

4. To get your tumblebug tumbling, place it at the top of a board propped up at a 30° angle (this is a gentle slope). Watch it fly down the runway!

Did you know?
There are more insect species than there are bird, fish, reptile, amphibian, and mammal species combined. Entomologists, people who study insects, have identified almost one million different types of insects. Some people think there may actually be three times that number!

TWO BY TWO

You could easily make an arkful of animals using this construction method. Paint your animals as realistically as you want or invent some wild and crazy creatures all your own!

SLOTTED CARD-BOARD ANIMALS

Poster board, about 11″ × 17″

Scissors
Paint or markers

Note The instructions here are for four-legged animals, but you can easily make creatures with more legs.

This horse looks much like those the Chinese traditionally paint and sculpt. Have you ever seen any pictures of them? They have very fat bodies and delicate heads and feet. In fact, one of the most famous cave paintings is the one in Lascaux, France known as the "Chinese horse," because it looks so much like Chinese paintings of horses.

When you're not tossing your bean bag around, use it as a paperweight.

1. Draw the outlines of both the animal's body and two sets of legs on the poster board. If you want your animal to have a separate tail, draw that, too.

2. Cut all the pieces out. Now cut inch-long slits in the legs, tail, and body. Do this by cutting a narrow "V," no wider than the thickness of the poster board.

3. Paint the animal any way you like. You may find it easier to do this before you put the animal together, but since each piece is painted on both sides, you can paint the assembled animal to save time.

Variations on a Theme

To make sturdier (and larger) animals, use wood instead of cardboard. Masonite, particle board, and plywood are good choices. Use a coping saw to cut out the shapes. Just remember to make the slits as wide as the board's thickness. Sand all rough edges before painting.

TURTLE TOSS

Sturdy turtle bean bags like these can stand a lot of rough play, so have fun tossing them back and forth or through a hole cut into a piece of cardboard.

FELT BEAN BAG
Green felt, about ¼ yard
Dried beans, peas, or rice
Needle and thread
Acrylic paints or permanent markers

Note This makes a bean bag that measures about 6″ across.

1. Sketch the outline of a turtle on a piece of paper. Make it a simple shape as shown. Make the outline about ½″ bigger than you want the final bean bag to be. Cut out the turtle shape.

CUTTING LINE

2. Fold the felt in half and pin the paper shape to it. Cut around the paper. Remove the paper pattern and stitch the two felt pieces together with small even stitches (leave a ½″ seam allowance). Leave a 2″ opening in the bag.

Leave 2″ opening

3. Turn the fabric right side out. Fill the turtle with beans, then sew the opening shut. Give the turtle some features and markings with paint or markers.

Decorate with paint or markers

Did you know?
The turtle is the only reptile that has a shell. There are 240 species of turtles in the world, 50 of which can be found in North America.

Felt is a type of unwoven cloth. Wool, fur, and combinations of other matted fibers are "felted" by steaming them under pressure. Most craft felt is made from rayon and acrylic fibers; real fur and wool felts are used to make hats, slippers, and other items.

A STITCH IN TIME

Basic sewing is a skill anyone can acquire. Knowing how to thread a needle and make a running stitch opens up a whole world of art projects to you.

Use a medium-sized needle with a big enough eye (opening) to thread easily. Cut a length of thread about 30″ long. Thread one end through the needle's eye; bring the two ends of the thread together and knot them. An easy way to do this is to wrap the ends around your index finger once; then use your thumb to roll the thread right off your finger. As you do so, the end will tangle itself and you can pull down on the thread to make the knot.

This creates a double thread that is nice and strong, and that won't slip out of the needle by mistake.

A running stitch is a basic sewing stitch. It is used for sewing two pieces of fabric together (usually right sides facing). Make a series of "dashes" by inserting the needle into both layers of fabric from the top and bringing it back up 1/4″ — 1/2″ from the first hole. Pull the thread all the way through. Continue in this way until you reach the end of your sewing.

Now work your way back to the beginning, filling in the empty spaces between the first stitches.

Make a knot in the thread where the sewing ends. Snip the excess thread.

Tip A 30″ thread doubled over and knotted ends up being only about 14″ long. This is an easy length to handle. While it's tempting to make your sewing thread longer (so you don't have to thread the needle as often), longer threads tend to get tangled and end up being more work.

Sewing was done by hand until the 1800s. In 1846, an American inventor named Elias Howe took out a patent for a sewing machine he invented.

BUTTERFLUTTER

The Cuna Indians of San Blas, off the coast of Panama, create a unique art with brightly-colored fabric. You can make similar *molas,* as these panels are called, using colored paper.

Mola panels are traditionally sewn onto blouses. In fact, the word *mola* means "blouse" in the Cuna language, but it is commonly used to refer to the panels themselves.

PAPER *MOLA*
Colored paper, 4 colors about 8½″ × 11″
Scissors
X-acto knife
White glue

1. Choose which color you want to show up the most. On this sheet, draw the outline of an animal, such as this butterfly, or any one you like. Make the shape slightly oversized. Around it draw lots of short, thick, rounded lines as shown.

2. Cut out all the shapes (use the scissors for the large shape, and the X-acto knife for the smaller shapes).

3. Place this cut out paper over one of the other colored sheets. With a pencil, draw a faint outline on the second sheet about ¼″ from the cut shape of the butterfly. Cut the second sheet along this line.

¼″

4. Do the same again with the third sheet of colored paper. Add more detail to this sheet.

5. Sandwich all the layers together, starting with the fourth sheet that is not cut. On top of this place the third sheet you cut, then the second, and lastly, the

first. Glue the four layers together in their proper order.

Tip You can add even more colors to your *mola* by slipping small scraps of paper under any of the layers that are cut out. Glue or tape them in place.

Variations on a Theme
Use colored rectangles of felt to make a *mola*. Sketch your design on a sheet of tracing paper first; then transfer it to the felt. If you find it hard to cut the felt with an X-acto knife, cut the shapes out with sharp scissors, after first slitting the felt with the knife.

Red is one of the most common colors used in *molas*. Use it and a combination of bright colors such as shocking pink, emerald green, royal blue, sunny yellow, and even black for a design in authentic colors.

IVY LEAGUE

This songbird may not awaken you with its singing, but it will certainly brighten a windowsill. In about six weeks time, ivy will completely cover the wire frame of this charming chirper.

TOPIARY BIRD

Wire, such as 14- or 16-gauge wire, about 52" long
Wire cutters
Pliers
Twist ties
Waterproof tape
Small stones or gravel
Ivy plant, growing in a 4" pot

1. Cut a piece of wire about 42" long. Bend it into the bird shape shown or into your own shape. The base of this bird takes about 8" of wire, the central "stem" another 8", and the bird itself the remaining wire. Fasten the end of the wire to the central stem with a twist tie.

Don't worry if the wire has any kinks or bends—the ivy will eventually cover them.

2. For a fuller, more three-dimensional shape, add a 10" circle of wire to the mid-section, as shown. Attach it with twist ties. Cover the entire frame with waterproof tape.

3. Remove the ivy plant from the pot by holding it upside-down and giving it a shake. The plant should drop out, soil and all.

4. Place the frame in the pot. Anchor it with some small rocks; then replace the ivy plant and its soil. Start training the plant right away by wrapping a long piece of ivy around the central stem and up to the bird shape.

5. Keep the plant in a bright spot, but away from direct sunlight (you can keep it in a windowsill but make sure it's facing north or east). Turn the plant now and again, so that it grows evenly on all sides.

Trim the plant as it grows. Wherever you cut a stem, it will branch off into two stems, which is the trick to getting the ivy to completely cover the frame.

Water the plant when the soil feels dry, but don't overwater it. Give the ivy a dose of fertilizer every month, and it should live a long, happy life.

Variations on a Theme
A topiary bird is only one of

Ask for one of these varieties of English ivy at your local garden center. They are perfect for portable topiary such as you've made.

- Itsy Bitsy
- Shamrock
- Duck Foot
- Fiesta
- Lustrous Carpet

▶

The art of shaping plants into animals and other objects dates from about 100 B.C. Well-to-do Romans livened up the gardens of their country estates with all sorts of unusual shapes.

many fantastic forms topiary can take. Bend some wire into any animal or shape you can think of.

You can also make topiary forms outdoors. Make a frame similar to the one shown here, or clip an existing bush (ask permission first!) into a surprising shape.

People who grow herbs sometimes include in their gardens a design known as a *knot*. Low-growing plants are planted in intertwining patterns, such as the one shown here.

The different greens of the different herbs make knot gardens particularly effective. You can make a type of knot garden yourself by planting various compact flowers in interesting patterns.

SNOW SNAKE

Most snakes hibernate in winter, but not this one!
This snake looks forward to a good, wet snow, when it can
slither down a hill. Get your friends together to play
this Iroquois Indian game.

PAINTED SNOW SNAKE

Straight branch, at least 4 feet long (see *Note*)
Short screws
Washers, to fit screws
Sandpaper
Acrylic paints

Note If you can't find a branch, you can use an old broom handle, some quarter-round molding from the lumberyard, or a length of wood, ripped to size.

1. If you are using a branch, peel off the bark. This is easy to do with dead branches. The wood will probably be satiny-smooth but sand any rough spots. If you are using purchased wood, round off any sharp corners and sand the wood smooth.

▶

2. Attach the washers to one end of the branch with the screws. Place them on either side of the wood like eyes. These serve to weight the stick so that it travels faster.

3. Paint designs on your snake. This isn't strictly necessary, but it makes it easier to identify your own snake. Some of the traditional Iroquois designs used in their art are shown on this page.

4. The rules of the game are simple. Find a nice, steep, snow-covered hill. First prepare a track by dragging a log through the snow; pack the snow down firmly. Make a lip along the sides so the snakes won't fly off the track. One by one, send the snakes down the hill. The one that travels farthest wins.

Many scientists believe snakes evolved from lizards millions of years ago, as snakes resemble lizards more than any other of the reptiles. Unlike lizards, snakes lack legs, movable eyelids, and outer ears. There are 2,700 kinds of snakes worldwide.

The Iroquois Indians were comprised of many tribes, including the Mohawk, Oneida, Onondaga, Cayuga and Seneca. The Iroquois name for themselves was *Ongwanonhsiono* which means "we long house builders."

For another Iroquois Indian craft you can make, see the felt moccasins on page 148.

Did you know?
Because snakes are cold-blooded, they are unable to survive in the polar regions and in higher elevations. There are no snakes, however, in Ireland and New Zealand.

THE PORTRAIT GALLERY

It was a long time before artists learned to draw people. It's not that the human figure is hard to draw, it's just that our superstitious ancestors were afraid of capturing their own spirits if they drew themselves! Luckily, people figured out that portraits didn't cast spells. And because of this, we know how the Egyptians, ancient Greeks, and Chinese people looked, how they dressed, and what they did for work and play. We also have an idea of how they felt about themselves. Portraits have helped us understand people from long ago right up to the present day.

ME, MYSELF & I

When you're looking for someone to draw or paint, you can always choose yourself. Work from memory or set up a mirror and seat yourself in front of it.

SELF–PORTRAIT

Paper or canvas
Pencils, paint, or markers
Mirror

Note Keep in mind that a mirror reverses images. This doesn't matter much in portraiture, but you may be surprised when you look at your self-portrait to discover that your hair is parted on the wrong side!

1. Think about what you want your self-portrait to "say" about you. Do you want to make a realistic rendering of your face or are you interested in painting a picture of yourself at work or play? You can work out the details by spending some time sketching yourself in different poses or from different angles.

2. Lightly sketch in the outlines on the paper or canvas itself. Paint or color in the portrait as you like.

Add some detail to the background or highlight your face against a dark, plain background.

PENCIL POINTERS

Pencils are an indispensable tool for artists. They are perfect for everything from marking measurements to sketching with.

Pencils come in varying degrees of hardness. You are probably familiar with the different hardnesses writing pencils come in, such as No. 2 and No. 3. Artists' pencils are graded on a different system. They range from 8B, the softest, to 10H, the hardest (some manufacturers use yet another numbering system). There are at least 18 different hardnesses!

The softer pencils make a darker line that is easy to erase, but also smudges easily. (Drawings done in the softer leads should be sprayed with a fixative.) The harder leads hold a sharp point better, so they are good for detailed work. They make a grey-er line that doesn't erase easily, especially when you press down hard when you're drawing.

Soft and hard pencils used in combination, can create a variety of effects. For instance, a landscape might work well using soft pencils for the foreground, and hard ones (using light pressure) for the distant background. (See page 108 for more on creating perspective.)

▶

The Story of Art
Many artists throughout history have painted their own portraits, but none are as amazing as those painted by Rembrandt, a Dutch artist.

Rembrandt Harmenszoon van Rijn was born in 1606, and by the time he was in his twenties, he was a well-established artist. While he painted other people's portraits to make a living, he found time to paint over 60 of himself before he died in 1669.

For hints on proper proportion in figure drawing, see page 69.

PENCIL POINTERS, CONT.

Experiment with a medium-soft pencil such as a 2B (perhaps the most common for sketching) on different paper surfaces. Slightly textured paper works well, but you can have fun drawing on very rough paper, such as watercolor paper, as well as smoother stock.

One of the nice things about pencils, of course, is that lines can be erased and reworked. The standard rubber eraser (the kind found on the ends of writing pencils) is good for general erasing, but you can get better results erasing small areas, if you use a kneaded eraser or the relatively new plastic or vinyl erasers.

KNEADED ERASER

Artists traditionally make detailed pencil drawings of paintings they later execute in oil. The pencil drawings are every bit as expressive and beautiful as the full-color, finished paintings.

ALL TOGETHER

Before the camera was invented, artists were commissioned to paint portraits, and many of these were group portraits. You be the artist and paint a portrait of your schoolmates, your family, or any group you want.

GROUP PORTRAIT

Long roll of wide paper, such as newsprint
Pencil, paint, or markers

Note If you don't have a continuous sheet of paper, tape individual sheets together at the back, to make a piece as long as you need.

1. Think about how you want to group all the people in your portrait. If you have the space to show each full-figure, you can have everyone lined up single file.

If you'd rather show a group assembled around a table, for instance, or a campfire, or on the playground, plan your composition to include everything you want.

2. Make plenty of sketches of the group before setting out to make a final portrait. You don't want to forget anyone! Spend some time planning the picture so that it is balanced (not everyone should be huddled on one side of the paper, for instance), and so that each person is clearly defined.

3. Complete the portrait by painting all the large areas and then all the details. If you are painting a lot of people, emphasize the notable details only, so the painting won't be too busy.

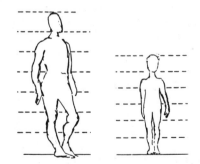

WELL–PROPORTIONED

Here are a few tricks you can use to make your portraits a little more realistic. These proportions work for figures seen from the front (change the proportions slightly for figures seen from different angles, to make them appear more natural).

The human head can generally be divided into three parts. From the top of the head to the top of the eyebrows is one; from eyebrows to bottom of the nose another; and from nose to the bottom of the chin a third.

The width of the nose is roughly equal to the width of one eye, and the mouth is just a bit wider.

Children's heads can be divided into just two parts. Their eyes appear larger, while their noses and mouths seem smaller.

The body, too, can be marked off into sections. If you count the head as one, an adult figure is about seven heads tall. But a 1-year-old is only four heads tall; a 4-year-old, five heads; a 9-year-old, six heads.

Similarly, a young child's arms might be about two heads long, but a full-grown man's arms are easily three heads long.

MR. SANDMAN

The Navajo Indians of Arizona and New Mexico create sandpaintings that often include figures from their religion as part of healing rituals. You can make your own sand portraits using a similar technique.

The Story of Art
The sandpaintings the Navajos make are not permanent paintings. A patch of bare ground is cleared inside a hogan, the traditional Navajo adobe building, and sand is carefully poured into intricate designs right on the ground. The sandpaintings are always destroyed as part of the healing ceremony.

The Navajos are thought to have learned the art of sandpainting from the Pueblo Indians. They, in turn, are said to have learned it from the Spanish who first came upon the southwestern part of the United States in the mid-16th century.

SANDPAINTING

Clean, sifted sand, about 1 shovelful
Colored powders, such as powdered poster paints, ground spices, corn meal, crushed charcoal
Stiff cardboard, about 8½″ × 11″
White glue

Note Some of the finely-ground spices and powdered paints can make you sneeze! Mix them with the sand carefully, so that the fine particles won't irritate your nose.

1. Make an assortment of colored sands by mixing various powders with small amounts of sand. (You can use some of the coarser powders, such as corn meal, by themselves.) Real Navajo sandpaintings are made with earth colors, such as tans and browns, brick red, soft yellow, and turquoise. Leave a portion of the sand untinted for the background.

2. Brush slightly watered-down glue over the entire piece of cardboard, and sprinkle it with plain sand. Give the cardboard a tap to shake off any loose grains.

3. "Paint" designs directly on the background with glue. Squirt it from the bottle for fine lines; use a brush to fill in larger areas. Do one color at a time, sprinkling the sand in place while the glue is still wet.

Use the picture here to guide you or make up your own designs.

Tip With normal handling, some of the sand may work loose and fall off. To prevent this, you can spray the painting with a matte fixative. Be sure to do this outdoors to avoid breathing the fumes.

TRADITIONAL SYMBOLS

SUN

LIGHTNING

CORN

SNAKE

Instead of preparing your own background, use a sheet of purchased sandpaper. This comes in a variety of colors, from the charcoal grey of emery paper to the reddish sand of garnet paper.

You can dig your own sand down by the beach (if it's your own property), or you can purchase it from a sand and gravel pit or a lumberyard (the latter sells it by the bag).

SHADOW SHOW

People have been making puppets for thousands of years, and shadow puppets are among the oldest. Simple silhouetted figures can be glued to long sticks or straws, but puppets with movable parts are even more fun to use.

SHADOW PUPPETS

Poster board, about 9″ × 12″, per puppet
Scissors
X-acto knife
Hole puncher
4 paper fasteners, per puppet
2 wire coat hangers, per puppet
Wire cutters
Pliers
Tape

Note The instructions here are for a male figure with arms that bend at the shoulder and elbow. Adapt the instructions to make other figures, including animals that have moving arms, legs, or heads.

1. Sketch the outline of your figure on the poster board. (You can do this on a separate piece of paper first, if you prefer, and transfer the outline to the poster board.) It must be large enough so that the shoulder and elbow joints are at least ½″ wide (to accomodate the paper fasteners). Notice how the shoulders of the figure shown here are very broad, and how the arms are made in two parts.

2. Cut the figure out with a pair of scissors. Use the X-acto knife to cut out any interior sections, such as the eye, ear, and buttons of this figure.

3. Punch holes in the shoulders and in the shoulder and elbow joints of the two arms. Fasten them together with the paper fasteners. Make sure the fasteners aren't pressed down too hard against the poster board—there should be a little play so that the joints bend easily.

Cut here

Cut the paper fasteners with the wire cutters, so that they don't show when the arms are moved about.

4. Cut a wire coat hanger (snip off the bent hook completely) the length of the puppet plus about 8″. Bend it with the pliers so that it conforms to the figure. Tape the wire in place with short lengths of tape.

Instead of taping the wire to the back of the puppet, you can sew it in place. Use strong thread such as carpet or buttonhole thread, and stitch right through the poster board and around the wire to hold it in place.

▶

The Story of Art
The best known shadow puppets and plays are those from Java. There are over 600 different characters used to tell various legends and stories that have been handed down for centuries.

The Javanese puppets are called *wayangs*, and they are made from thin buffalo skins, chiseled and punched into intricate designs. The puppets are brightly colored on both sides. Size plays an important part in identifying characters. The ogres are large with rounded eyes and blunt features. The heroes are always small, slender figures with downcast eyes. In the enacted stories, the heroes always conquer their larger foes by means of cunning and thoughtful actions.

5. Cut two wires for the arms from the other coat hanger. They should be about 18″ long, or long enough so that you can raise the puppet's arms high, but still have your hands hidden. Wrap some tape around one end of each wire several times; then tape the wires to the puppet's hands.

6. Use the puppet behind a lit screen. See *Shadow Screen* for hints on making your own.

Variations on a Theme
If you would prefer to use a traditional open puppet stage instead of a lit screen, color the puppets on the side that faces the audience.

SHADOW SCREEN

Shadow puppets are most effective when they are lit from behind, so that the silhouettes really stand out. For the large, jointed figures, stretch a white sheet across a doorway. Create a barrier to hide behind, out of cardboard or an overturned table. Place a lamp or a powerful flashlight at puppet-level; put it on a table or pedestal far enough behind you so that you have room to manipulate the figures.

Smaller figures can be placed behind a table-top screen made from cardboard and translucent paper such as parchment (ask for large sheets of parchment at an art store). Use a small lamp to light the screen.

TABLE-TOP SCREEN

Put on your shadow plays in a darkened room for the best results.

Make a stand to hold several puppets when you are putting on a show. Stick the body wires into a thick piece of styrofoam, or drill some holes in a block of wood to stand the puppets in.

A SHOW OF HANDS

Hand puppets are great fun to use, but have you ever made your own puppets with papier-mâché heads? With this simple paper pulp method, you can model the heads for a whole cast of characters!

PAPIER–MÂCHÉ HAND PUPPETS

Papier-mâché pulp (see page 74)
Poster board, about 3″ × 5″
Tape
Narrow-necked bottle, such as a ketchup bottle
Acrylic paints
Felt or other sturdy fabric, about ¼ yard
Needle and thread
White glue

1. Have a batch of papier-mâché pulp ready. Tape the piece of poster board into a tube (along the 5″ side). Make it so it fits over the neck of the bottle you are using. The tube is the neck support for the puppet's head, and the bottle becomes a handy holder.

2. Using the pulp like clay, mold a head right onto the poster board neck. Build out features such as a nose, eyebrows, mouth, and chin. Attach ears and hair, if you like. Make the features prominent for the best results. Set aside in a safe, warm place to dry for 5–7 days.

3. When the head is completely dry, paint it with acrylic paints. Cover the entire head to protect it from moisture. Add painted features and hair, or make hair from yarn or fake fur.

4. Make a glove for the puppet's body. First make a pattern. On a piece of paper, place your hand in the position shown. Draw the outline of a glove around it. See how your thumb and littlest finger fit into the arms, and your index finger extends up into the neck. Make the outline ½″ larger all the way around for the sewing seam. Cut out the pattern.

5. Pin the paper pattern onto a piece of felt folded in half. Cut out two glove pieces. Remove the pattern and sew the glove together (right-sides facing), leaving both the neck and the bottom open. Turn the glove right-side out.

Leave open

You can use sandpaper to smooth any rough edges on your puppet's head. Give the entire head a sanding for a different look.

Did you know?
Papier-mâché is French for "chewed-up paper"!

▶

The Story of Art
Hand puppets date from about the 17th century. Most had carved wooden heads and hands, and cloth bodies. Traveling puppeteers set up mobile stages or performed from the backs of wagons. The plays usually poked fun at local gossip or politics. Some puppet shows featured Punch and Judy, a quarreling husband and wife who often came to comical blows.

So what do English people call what we know as corn? Maize.

6. Insert the head into the glove neck and glue it in place. Add fabric trims, buttons, and felt hands to the puppet body, if you like.

PAPIER-MÂCHÉ PULP

Papier-mâché pulp, or mash as it is sometimes called, is a terrific modeling material. Use it to make puppet heads and to add dimension to papier-mâché masks. The recipe here makes about 1½ cups pulp.

Fill a medium-sized bowl about half full with scrap paper torn into small pieces. You can use newspaper, computer printout paper, old letters and envelopes—any paper that isn't shiny. Pour boiling water over the paper (have an adult help you with this), so that the paper is completely covered. Let soak for 1 hour.

Meanwhile, measure 2 heaping tablespoons flour and put it into a small saucepan. Add ½ cup water and stir until well blended. Cook this mixture on the stove, stirring constantly, for about 3 minutes, or until it has come to a boil and is thick (have your adult friend help you again). Set aside to cool.

When the paper has soaked long enough, put small handfuls of it into a blender, adding plenty of extra water to each batch. Blend on high for about 15 seconds. Pour the pulp into a colander. Continue in this way until all the paper has been reduced to pulp.

Squeeze as much water from the pulp as you can. Measure 1 cup of the pulp (pack it into the measuring cup) and place it in a bowl. To this, add the cooled flour paste. Mix well with your hands.

HARVEST HELP

In England, where corn refers to any grain, such as wheat, rye, or oats, good luck harvest figures called corn dollies are made each year. You can make your own from what we call corn in this country.

CORNHUSK FIGURE

Corn husks, fresh or dried, about 6–8 pieces
String
Cotton balls, about 4
Scraps of cloth, yarn, beads, and pipe cleaners (optional)

Note If you are using dried husks, soak them in water to soften them. Fresh husks need no special preparation.

1. Take a strip of husk and place a few cotton balls in the middle, twisting and tying it with string to make a head.

Make some arms by folding another husk and tying it near each end to make hands. Slip the arms between the husks that extend under the head. Tie the waist with string.

2. Arrange enough husks around the figure's waist so that they overlap slightly. Tie them in place with string.

3. Fold the husks down carefully. For a woman wearing a long skirt, cut the husks straight across at the hem. To make a man, divide the skirt husks in two and tie each

half at the ankles. Let the figure dry completely.

4. You can leave your figure as is, or give it a face, hair, or even some fancier clothes. Use a fine-tipped marker to draw facial features. Glue some fuzzy yarn on for hair. Add some tiny beads for buttons, and bits of fabric for aprons or vests. A pipe cleaner staff or cane will help the man stand upright.

Although they are still called corn dollies, many English harvest decorations are made in shapes such as spiraling ribbons or braided strips.

GOOD SPIRITS

Not all dolls are meant to be played with. The Kachina dolls made by the Pueblo Indians of New Mexico are used to teach religion. Real Kachinas are carved from wood, but you can make your own from cardboard tubes and glue.

KACHINA FIGURE
Cardboard tubes, from paper towels, toilet tissue, mailing tubes, and coat hangers (see *Note*)
Handsaw or serrated kitchen knife
Scissors
White glue
Paint
Fabric scraps and feathers

Note Make your own tubes, if you like, by rolling up pieces of thin cardboard, such as poster board, and gluing or taping them.

1. The Kachina figure shown here is just one of many different types that are made. Some carved Kachinas have movable arms; others wear cloth kilts or blankets over their shoulders. Use the design shown here or come up with your own (study the pictures in books for authentic designs—your library should have some books).

2. Make the figure's body from one of the larger tubes. Use the handsaw or the serrated knife to saw it to the size you want. To make the legs, cut out two narrow panels, front and back, on one end.

Kachina dolls represent male dancers known as Kachinas, who themselves represent supernatural beings in the various Pueblo religions.

▶

Traditional Kachina dolls are carved from the dried roots of cottonwood trees.

3. Use the narrower tubes for the arms, ears, and nose. Glue these in place. Cut a headdress from a flat piece of cardboard and attach it by fitting it into small slits, cut into the body tube at the head end.

4. Paint the Kachina figure in traditional earth colors or any way you like. Glue on fabric pieces and feathers, if you wish.

Some traditional Pueblo symbols include

 RAINBOW SUN

STAR   CLOUDS

 LIGHTNING

OTHER SELVES

You can be anyone (or anything!) you like when you're hiding behind a mask. Here are two ideas for masks you can make. The first is a quick, colorful mask meant to be worn; the second looks like it might have come straight from a tribal ceremony.

Some masks are simply painted on. In many cultures, face-painting is used to identify tribes, but it is also used to work magic. Of course, painting one's face is also a way to beautify it. Women all over the world use make-up.

CARDBOARD MASK
Corrugated cardboard, about 7″ × 11″
Poster board, about 5″ square
Scissors
X-acto knife
Paint, colored paper, yarn, glitter, feathers
White glue
Hole puncher
¼″ elastic, about 8″ long

Note For best results, cut the corrugated cardboard so that the corrugated channels run the short way. That way you can easily bend the cardboard to conform to your face.

1. Ease the cardboard into a gentle arc by bending it inch by inch along the channels.

2. Have someone measure the distance between your two eyes, from pupil to pupil. Mark where the eye holes should go on the cardboard, placing them about 2″ from the top edge. Cut out the holes.

3. Make a triangular hole for your nose. Then cut a nose out of the poster board, in the shape shown

here. Fold the nose down the center, fold in the tabs, and glue the nose in place on the mask. Cut a hole for your mouth.

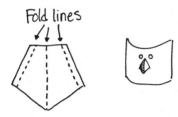

Fold lines

4. Decorate the mask any way you like. Use the paint, paper, yarn, and assorted trims to create a colorful mask. Punch holes for the elastic on either side, tie on the elastic, and try on for size.

PAPIER–MÂCHÉ MASK

Corrugated cardboard, about 3″ × 24″
Stapler
Newspaper
¼ cup flour
Saucepan
Paint
Yarn, beads, and other trims

Note This mask can be made to be worn, if you make the oval ring large enough to fit around your face and poke holes for your eyes and nose, and for an elastic band.

1. Ease the strip of corrugated cardboard into an oval shape and staple the ends together. Crumple up some newspaper and stuff it into the oval, up to the level of the cardboard.

SIDE VIEW

2. Make the flour and water paste. Mix ¼ cup flour with 4 cups of water in a medium-sized saucepan. Bring to a boil on the stove (ask an adult to help you), stirring until the mixture is smooth and the consistency of cream. Set aside to cool.

3. Meanwhile, tear some newspaper into short strips. Save some whole sheets to crumple and twist into shapes to build up the features of your mask. When the paste is cool enough to work with, paste down the strips and twists to make the mask's face. Overlap the strips, and smooth them out with your hands as you lay them down to avoid wrinkles and bumps.

4. The entire mask should have four to five layers of strips. It's a good idea to put down two layers and let them dry before adding the next two. The final layer can be made with tissue paper or another thin paper, if you like.

5. Remove the crumpled-up paper that is stuffed inside the oval. Let the mask dry for an additional few days, until there is no hint of moisture. Paint the mask a rich brown to look like wood, or paint it any way you like. Add some extra touches, such as the red tongue shown here, and the matted hair made from yarn.

Masks have long been used in theater. Ancient Greek actors wore masks to convey emotions as well as different characters. Today, masks are still used in traditional Japanese Noh plays, and actors in India and China paint their faces to resemble masks. Can you think where you might have seen painted face-masks? The circus, that's where!

Tribal masks are used for special ceremonies and dances. A mask is sometimes used to hide the wearer from evil; it is sometimes used to frighten away ghosts. Sometimes masks are used as disguises so that people can summon spirits without being recognized.

THE THIRD DIMENSION

What makes a sculpture different from a painting or a print?
The fact that it is not flat but has a third dimension that you
can touch gives sculpture its own place in the art world.
You can view some sculpture from all sides, either walking
around large pieces on the ground, or holding the smaller
ones in your hand. Some sculptures are meant to hang on a
wall and be viewed from the front and sides only. Some pieces
even hang from the ceiling, and others, like kites, know no
bounds!

WHITTLE AWHILE

Have you ever pared an apple with a knife? Then you can carve soap to make a sculpture. A bar of soft soap is perfect for beginning whittlers and advanced ones alike.

SOAP CARVING

| Bar of soft soap, such as Ivory® |
| Paring knife or jack knife (see *Note*) |
| Pencil |

Note You can also use a table knife for carving, but the sharper knives, such as those listed above, are easier to work with. Handle any knife with care.

1. Make several sketches of your sculpture on a piece of paper, before you begin carving. Draw what you want the sculpture to look like from the front, back, top, and sides. Make your sketches the actual size of the bar of soap. The sketches shown here are for a bear.

FRONT   BACK

SIDE

TOP

2. With the pencil, carefully draw the outlines directly on the soap.

3. Holding the soap firmly in one hand, start carving the soap outside the outlines. Brace your thumb against the soap, and cut slowly and carefully towards yourself. This really is the safest way to handle the knife. You have more control, and if you take small slices, there is little danger you will cut yourself.

4. Take your time. Remember you can always take away more of the soap, but you can't replace what you've already carved. Whittle away the soap from all the different angles. Use a pencil, or linoleum cutting tools to add various textures or to gouge out parts of the soap. To smooth the surface, hold the knife blade at a 90° angle and scrape the soap by pulling the knife towards yourself.

5. For a final smoothing, wet the soap and rub it gently with a soft cloth. Let the sculpture dry for several days before handling it.

Tip Keep your knife as clean as possible. The soft soap slivers will cling to it, making carving difficult. Scrape the soap off now and again with another knife or against a piece of scrap wood.

Sculptors who carve their work have many materials to choose from. There's wood, ivory, and any number of types of stone, from marble to jade.

This small animal figure is very similar to the carved pieces made by the Eskimos. The Eskimos make their carvings out of a soft stone called soapstone (steatite). This is a recent trend in Eskimo art. Originally, the Eskimos carved only walrus tusks and bone.

►

Did you know?
Marble sculptures made in ancient Greece and Rome were painted with bright colors. It's hard to imagine what they looked like because we are so used to seeing the marble statues unpainted.

CHIP OFF THE OLD BLOCK

For something a little different, you might want to try your hand at sculpting with plaster of Paris.

Plaster of Paris comes as a powder that you mix with water (follow the instructions on the box) and pour into containers such as milk cartons or shoe boxes. You can also pour it into plastic bags or in holes made in sand to create free-form pieces.

Vary the texture of the plaster by adding such things as coffee grounds or vermiculite (ask for this at a garden center) to the mix. These happen to make the plaster a little easier to carve as well.

Plaster of Paris sculpting is a messy business. First of all, it's best to mix your plaster in disposable containers, and never, never dump any plaster down the drain. It will harden and clog the drain. Secondly, the plaster raises a lot of dust while you're carving and chipping away at it, so make sure to cover your work area and clean up after yourself. Dipping the block of plaster in water every now and again helps to keep the dust down and may make carving a bit easier. Use a chisel or a flat-head screwdriver and a hammer to chip away at the block. Other workshop and kitchen tools you can use include metal files, nails, and old kitchen knives.

PAT IT & PRICK IT

Salt dough is one of the easiest materials to model with, and it doesn't require any special equipment to make it hard. Just pop your sculptures in the oven, or let them air dry.

The earliest sculpted pieces we know of were carved ivory and stone figures, known as fertility figures. These were supposed to bring good luck to women of child-bearing age.

SALT DOUGH SCULPTURE

Salt dough (see page 81)
Acrylic paints
Clear nail polish or other varnish

1. Have a batch of salt dough ready. Keep what you aren't using at the moment in a plastic bag or covered bowl.

2. The items shown here are just a few of the possible things you can do with salt dough. The rabbit is made by rolling out the dough and cutting it with a cookie cutter. The eye is simply a tiny ball of dough placed in position and poked with a toothpick. The fur is made by pressing the tines of a fork into the dough in a random pattern.

ADDING THE EYE

The braided napkin ring is made by braiding three ropes of dough together and wrapping them around a paper towel roll. The ends are wetted slightly and pinched together to secure them.

FORMING THE RING

The candle holder is made by cutting a circle of rolled-out dough and adding modeled pieces of dough all around it to build up the sides. Each little piece is brushed with water to help make it stick.

BRUSHING WITH WATER

3. You can let your sculpted pieces air dry, or you can bake them in the oven. Air-drying takes about 2–3 days, depending on how thick the sculpted pieces are. The pieces stay white when you dry them this way.

If you prefer to speed things up, you can bake the pieces in a 300°F oven for about an hour. The dough will turn a light brown. The dough should be firm when done, so check it after an hour and let it bake longer, if necessary. Let the pieces cool completely before handling them.

4. Seal your sculptures to protect them from moisture. You can paint the pieces with acrylics, in which case they need no other sealer (just make sure to cover the entire piece with the paint). Or you can varnish the salt dough sculptures with clear nail polish or another waterproof varnish.

For another use for salt dough, see *A-Tisket, A-Tasket* on page 131.

Variations on a Theme
Salt dough sculptures can be "finished" in a number of different ways. If you are baking your pieces, brush them with some egg yolk before putting them into the oven. This gives the pieces a golden brown color. Experiment with other finishes, such as staining the pieces with shoe polish or wood stain. (First seal the dry dough with a couple of coats of clear varnish, then stain the dough; rub off any excess with a soft cloth and brush on another coat of varnish.)

SALT DOUGH

This recipe makes enough salt dough for a dozen ornaments, several napkin rings, plenty of candle holders, and then some! You can make half as much dough for starters, if you like, by using just half the ingredients.

Mix 2 cups flour and 1 cup salt in a bowl. Slowly add 1 cup water, mixing it thoroughly. Knead the dough with your fingers for about 5 to 7 minutes. It shouldn't stick to the table; if it does, sprinkle a little flour on your work surface.

Keep the dough in a plastic bag or covered bowl, so that it won't dry out. The dough will keep for about 5 days.

Not all carvings are free-standing. Have you ever seen examples of *relief* work, perhaps as part of a building? This is done by cutting away parts of a flat surface so that the figures stand out from the background, but are still part of it. Depending on how deep or shallow the carving is, the relief is known as high or low (low relief work is usually known as *bas-relief,* after the French word for "low"). Much relief sculpture tells a story. The Egyptians used this story-telling technique, as did the Greeks.

HANG UPS

Not all sculptures are meant to sit solidly on the ground. Mobiles are hanging sculptures that move freely with the breeze or with the touch of your hands. Here are two types of hanging art you can make.

The Story of Art
In the 1930s, an American artist named Alexander Calder had an idea to hang a wire sculpture from the ceiling. He had seen how Chinese wind chimes moved with the breeze or with a push of the hand, and he wondered if large sculptures made from bent wires would do the same. The mobile was born!

SPIRAL MOBILE
Poster board, about 11″ square
Thin paper, 12 pieces about 4″ square
Pencil
Compass
Scissors
Needle and thread

Note The instructions here are for a mobile of hanging paper snowflakes. See *Variations on a Theme* for other things you might hang in this fashion.

1. Cut a 10″ circle out of the poster board. Use a compass to draw the circle or trace around a dinner plate with a pencil. Make a circle inside this one, about 1/2″ smaller. Cut it out. You now have a flat ring.

2. Pencil 12 dots around the ring, evenly spacing them. Poke four holes in the ring (placed between the pencil dots) and attach four pieces of thread to the ring. Make the threads about 18″ long; tie them together at the top so that the ring hangs level. Tack the ring up where you can reach it easily.

3. Cut 12 circles from the 12 pieces of thin paper. Use a compass to draw the circles or trace around a mug or drinking glass.

4. Fold one circle in half, then in thirds, and in half again. Use the scissors to snip little bits from the paper, on both sides, at the top and at the point. Open the paper, and there you have a 6-sided snowflake. Make 11 more snowflakes, altering the cuts so that each is slightly different.

5. Hang the snowflakes from the ring. Place one at each of the 12 dots. Let the first snowflake hang down about an inch from the ring. Have the second flake hang down about 2″ below the first; the third 2″ below the second, and so on. Hang the mobile high up.

Variations on a Theme

Hang other things from the ring, such as tiny birds made with tissue paper wings or stars cut from paper. Origami figures are also very effective grouped like this (see how to make flower blossoms from origami paper on page 94). You can also hang heavier items, if you start out with a sturdier ring. Look into using an embroidery hoop or a large plastic ring (the kind used for handbag handles) for this mobile.

The spiral is well represented in natural forms. From the unfurled fronds of ferns (these are called fiddleheads because they resemble the peg heads of violins!) to the inner chamber of the nautilus shell, there are many examples of spirals in nature.

FOUND TREASURE MOBILE

Feathers, shells, pieces of wood and bark, rocks, anything you can find!
Branches and twigs
Strong thread or fishing line

Note The mobile shown here is made from items collected outdoors, but you can also use bits and pieces of old toys, kitchen utensils, or what have you.

1. Gather up all your treasures to see what you have to work with.

2. Select a thick branch for the main cross piece, or use several thinner branches. Putting together a balanced mobile is an exercise in trial-and-error. You can't really know how everything will balance until you try, but that's part of the fun. Hang the mobile in a spot where you can easily reach it while you are working on it.

PIVOTAL POINT

Balance the mobile by adding (or taking away) weight from one part of a branch, or by moving items closer to (or farther from) the pivotal point.

3. Make sure all the knots you make in the string or fishing line are nice and tight. Hang the mobile in its permanent home, well out of the way of heads or leaping pets.

Make your own wind chimes using natural materials. Shells are a natural (no pun intended!). There's even a shell found on Atlantic beaches called the jingle shell, because it has such a nice tinkling sound. String up some hollow reeds or bamboo pieces for deeper sounding chimes. Just make sure you hang your material close together so that a slight breeze will set the chimes in motion to create the sound.

PARTY FAVORS

Piñatas can really liven up a party! Here's how to make your own in the traditional star shape. Fill it with candy or with individually-wrapped packages for all the guests at your next party.

The piñata originated in Italy in the 16th century. Just for fun, an earthenware pot called a *pignatta* was hung from a rope and swung at by a blindfolded person. The pot was not decorated nor did it have anything in it.

The custom made its way to Mexico, where the piñata became part of the Christmas celebration. It was only in this century that the piñata was gaily decorated with tissue paper and that papier-mâché was used as an alternative to an earthenware pot. Some Mexican piñatas are still made with a pot.

STAR PIÑATA

Large, round balloon
Newspaper
Flour, 1/4 cup
Saucepan
Strong string
Poster board, 6 pieces about 9″ square
Tissue paper, about 6-10 sheets
White glue
Candy or other treats

1. Blow up the balloon and tie it. Make some flour and water paste by mixing the 1/4 cup flour with 4 cups water in the saucepan. Stir well; bring to a boil on the stove (have an adult give you a hand), and cook until it is smooth and the consistency of cream. Set aside to cool.

2. Meanwhile, tear the newspaper into short strips. When the paste is cool enough to handle,

paste the strips to the balloon. Overlap them slightly. Cover the entire balloon with a single layer of strips.

3. Make a harness for the balloon. Tie two lengths of string into a cross and lay the balloon on top of it. Bring the four strands up over the sides of the balloon and tape them in place. Tie the strings together at the top.

4. Cover the balloon with at least three more layers of newspaper

strips. Hang the balloon to dry. This takes about 3-5 days.

5. Cut six shapes from the poster board, following the diagram shown, to make six cones. Glue the cone edges together.

NOTCH THIS EDGE

Glue the six cones to the balloon.

6. Cut the tissue paper into strips 3″ wide. Fold each strip in half length-wise, and make cuts in the folded edge every 1/4″, to within half an inch of the cut side. To speed things up, you can cut through four or five folded strips at a time.

MAKE CUTS EVERY 1/4″

7. Unfold each strip and refold it inside out so that the ruffles stand up. Glue the ruffles to the hanging piñata, making the strips conform to the piñata's shape (and working around the cones). Start at the top and work your way down. Place each row so that the ruffles cover the glued portion of the previous row.

8. Cut a small triangular trap door in the piñata by making two cuts and folding down the flap.

Pop the balloon and remove it. Fill the piñata with goodies; push the flap back in place.

Variations on a Theme
Piñatas come in all shapes and sizes. You can turn a round balloon form into a face (just add some papier-mâché features) or an animal (attach some legs).

Instead of covering the piñata with tissue paper ruffles, you can make the final layer of your piñata from white paper towels and finish it with whole sheets

of tissue paper glued down. Or paint the piñata with poster paints or acrylics.

Use your imagination to create some other piñata shapes. How about making a snake from a couple of long balloons laid end to end? For something really easy that would be perfect for your next birthday party, try this: wrap a square box with wrapping paper to look like a big present!

Tissue paper bleeds when it gets wet, so make sure you wear a smock or an apron when you are gluing the tissue ruffles in place.

For added decoration, glue or tape some long strands of tissue paper to each of the cones.

LET THERE BE LIGHT

Candles add a festive glow to the dinner table. Here are two simple candles you can make with ingredients found at your local supermarket or hardware store.

SAND–CAST CANDLE

Paraffin wax or old candles, about ½ pound
Crayons

Stub of an old candle
Sand, enough to fill a large bowl
Double boiler, or a saucepan and a bowl that fits over it

Note Wax is highly flammable. It must be melted over boiling water, and *never* directly in a pan set on top of the stove. Make sure you have an adult help you with this.

▶

The Story of Art
Tallow (fat from sheep and cows) and beeswax have been used in candlemaking since Roman times. Paraffin, which is distilled from wood, coal, and petroleum, was developed in the 19th century. Today, many candles are made from a combination of paraffin and beeswax.

This would be a great project to do down at a beach. Bring along a portable cookstove, but don't bother with the sand. You should find plenty there already!

1. In a large bowl (or in a sandbox), dampen some sand slightly so that you can dig a hole that keeps its shape. A hole about 4" deep and 4" across holds about half a pound of melted wax.

2. Place the candle stub in the hole so that the top is level with the top of the hole. Cut the stub shorter, if need be, or build up a little sand in the center of the hole to rest the candle on.

3. Cut the paraffin into small chunks and melt it in the top of the double boiler. Bring the water in the base to a boil. Keep an eye on the wax at all times (it may take as long as 15 minutes to melt ½ pound of wax). Have an adult help you at the stove. Color the wax with pieces of broken crayons (stir in only one or two to keep the color from getting muddy).

4. Carefully pour the wax into the hole. After about 15 minutes, poke a hole in the center of the candle, and pour in some more hot wax (wax shrinks as it cools, so you may have to do this again). Let the candle harden for several hours or overnight. Dig the candle out of the sand; brush off any loose grains. Level the bottom of the candle with a paring knife, if necessary.

LEVEL THE BOTTOM

EGG CANDLES
Eggs, as many as you like
Egg carton
Sharp pin
Nail scissors
Cooking oil
Small brush
Paraffin wax or old candles (see *Note*)
Crayons
String
Toothpicks
Double boiler, or a saucepan and a bowl that fits over it

Note A pound of paraffin fills about a dozen large eggshells.

1. First blow the eggs. To do this, poke a small hole at each end of an egg with a sharp pin. Thrust the pin deep into the holes to break the membrane. Holding the egg over a bowl, blow through one hole; the yolk and the white will come out the other.

2. Enlarge the hole at the narrow end of the egg with the nail scissors. Make the opening about 1" wide. Do as many shells as you need in this way. Wash the shells carefully and place them upside-down to dry. When they are dry, brush the insides of the eggs with cooking oil. Set the eggs in the egg carton.

3. Break the paraffin into small chunks and melt it in the top of the double boiler. (Have an adult help you at the stove, and remember that paraffin is flammable—see page 85). Color the wax with pieces of crayons (use only one or two crayons, or the wax will get muddy looking).

4. Cut the wicks for your candles. Cut the string into pieces about 5″ long. Lower the string halfway into the hot wax, one at a time; lift the string and wait a few seconds. Pull the string out straight while the wax is still soft.

5. With one hand, hold the wick upright in the shell. Carefully fill the shell up to the top with wax (have an adult pour the wax for you to make it easier). Anchor the wick between two toothpicks. Let set for 15 minutes.

6. Pierce a hole in the top of the candle and pour in more hot wax. (You may have to do this again as the candle cools.) Leave the candles for several hours or overnight, then peel away the shells. Trim the wicks, and level the bottoms of the candles with a paring knife.

Variations on a Theme
Give your candles a striped look. This is easily done. Fill the eggshells a third of the way up with one color. Let the wax harden for 15 minutes, then pour in more wax in a different color. Do this again with a third color.

You can either melt separate batches of wax for each color, or try this trick. Color the wax ini-

tially with just one light-colored crayon. Fill the shells part way. Then add a second crayon in a deeper shade to the wax in the double boiler. Stir well and pour a layer of this into the shells. Finally, add a dark crayon to the remaining wax and top off the shells with this color.

Put one of your egg-shaped candles in a pierced tin can lantern. See page 135 to learn how to make your own.

Tilt the eggshells slightly when you pour the first two layers. This gives the candles an interesting wavy look.

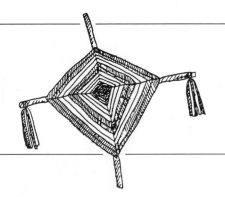

OJO DE DIOS

The *Ojo de Dios,* or God's Eye as it translates to English, is a traditional Mexican decoration that is thought to bring good luck. Maybe it will work for you!

The *Ojo de Dios* is traditionally displayed during the Green Squash Festival each October in Mexico.

GOD'S EYE

Yarn, in a variety of colors
2 straight twigs, 6″ to 10″ long

1. Make a cross with the twigs by placing one over the other. Lash the twigs together by wrapping yarn around them, first one way and then the other, until there's a nice, rounded hump that covers the twigs where they cross. This is the "eye."

▶

Make an *Ojo* from variegated yarn, which is already dyed several different colors. Or make your *Ojo* from short lengths of yarn you've dyed yourself. See page 147 for all you need to know to dye yarns with leaves, berries, and bark.

2. Bringing the yarn from behind, wrap it completely around one of the spokes of the cross. Carry the yarn to the next spoke and do the same. Continue in this way until the *Ojo* is as big as you like.

Change colors as you go, by tying new lengths of yarn. Try to make any color changes at the spokes, so that the knots are hidden at the back.

3. Finish the *Ojo* with a knot near one of the spokes. Add some tassels to the ends of the horizontal spokes, if you like. Tie a short length of yarn to the back for hanging the *Ojo*.

Variations on a Theme
For a more elaborate *Ojo,* add short twigs to the ends of any or all of the spokes, and make miniature *Ojos* at these points.

HIGH FLYER

You don't need to wait for a forecast of "high winds" to get this kite off the ground. This kite is as easy to launch as it is to make.

Kites are thought to have originated in China about 3,000 years ago.

PLASTIC BAG KITE
Plastic garbage bag, large kitchen size (13 gallon)
Scissors
Two 3/16″ dowels, 29″ long
Tape
Permanent markers, in assorted colors
String

Note You can use any plastic bag that's at least 23½″ × 29″

1. Spread the garbage bag flat on your work surface. Measure and mark the cutting lines as shown in the diagram (use any felt-tipped pen to mark the lines).

Folded edge of bag

10″

29″

6½″

5″

6″

12″

Cut along the lines, cutting away the shaded areas.

2. Open up the bag. Draw some features on the bag with the permanent markers. Take care not to smudge the markers before they have a chance to dry. Draw the traditional Japanese face shown here or decorate the kite any way you like.

3. Turn the kite over and tape the dowels in position. Use six pieces of tape for each dowel, as shown. Reinforce the corners of the cut-out and the wing tips with tape.

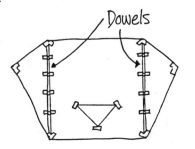

Dowels

4. Poke a tiny hole in each wing tip. Cut a piece of string ten feet long. Tie each end through the holes in the wing tips. This is the kite's bridle. Tie a loop at the end of the bridle. Attach the flying line (wrap lots of string around a piece of wood) to this loop.

MARK MAKERS

Felt-tip markers are a relatively recent development. They are very popular because they come in a rainbow of colors and are very easy to use.

There are two basic types of markers—permanent or waterproof markers, and water-based (sometimes called watercolor) markers. Permanent markers have the disadvantage of being slightly toxic and of staining clothes and skin. They are useful, however, wherever a waterproof drawing is needed. They do smear before they dry, especially when used on slick surfaces such as the plastic bag kite, so keep this in mind.

Water-based markers are safer to use but finished artwork must be protected from moisture.

These markers won't work on certain surfaces that repel the watery ink.

It's always a good idea to test your markers on a scrap of your material first. Permanent markers bleed quite a bit when used on porous paper, so be sure to protect your work surface with newspaper and keep in mind how the ink spreads outwards on the paper itself. If you are using permanent markers to color outlined artwork, save making the outlines until last. That way you can be sure the outlines really are on the outer edges of your drawings! Lightly pencil where the color is meant to go, color in the shapes, then come back with a water-based marker (or pen and ink) and make the outlines.

FLYING TIPS

The plastic bag described here is very easy to fly, even if you're on your own (many kites need two people to launch them, but not this one). All you need is a light, steady breeze (4–7 miles per hour is good—you can tell it's about right if you can feel the wind on your face and the leaves are rustling), and an open place away from power lines and trees.

Stand with your back to the wind and hold the kite up high with one hand. Let the line out as the kite tugs and climbs upward. If the kite dips down, let the line out a little more until the kite rights itself, then reel in the slack. If there doesn't seem to be any wind close to the ground, create your own by running with the kite until it's aloft.

WIND

Be sure to put the caps back on your markers when you are done using them; otherwise, they will dry out.

The Japanese make some enormous kites. In Hoshubana, kites are as large as 48 feet by 36 feet, with bridle lines 100 feet long! It takes as many as 50 grown men to get the kites up into the air.

We often refer to March as the kite flying month, but the gentle breezes of summer are often better than the gustier winds of spring.

PUZZLE PIECES

Most puzzles form a picture when you put the pieces together. Not this one! You have to break apart this Tangram square before you can make any pictures with its seven pieces.

The Tangram puzzle originated in China, where it's called *Chi-Chiao*. That's Chinese for "the seven clever pieces"!

TANGRAM

TANGRAM
Sturdy cardboard, 6″ square
Metal ruler
X-acto knife

Note The instructions here are for a Tangram measuring 6″ square. Follow the instructions to dissect a square of any size.

1. Mark the four corners of the cardboard with the letters A, B, C, and D, as shown.

2. Draw a line from D to B.

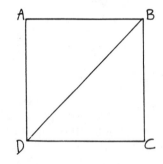

3. Make a mark halfway from A to B, and halfway from A to D. Draw a line connecting those two marks (this line is parallel to the one you made above).

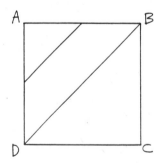

4. Place the ruler across A and C and draw a line from C up to the line you drew in step 3. Mark the very middle of the square with an O.

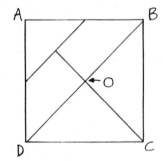

5. Make a mark halfway between D and O. Draw a line connecting that mark to the one halfway between A and D.

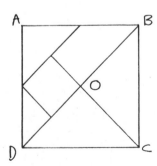

6. Make a mark halfway between B and O. Draw a line connecting that mark to the halfway mark of the line you made in step 3.

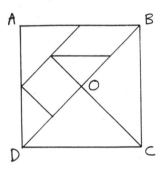

7. Using an X-acto knife, carefully cut along the lines. You now have seven puzzle pieces.

Scramble the puzzle pieces to create hundreds of different figures. Here's how to make a whale.

Here's how to make a sailboat.

How do you think you might make this dog?

The answer is shown upside-down. What other pictures can you make using all seven pieces?

Variations on a Theme
Your Tangram square doesn't have to be made out of thick cardboard. Cardboard is a good choice because the pieces hold up well and are easy to grasp, but experiment with other materials. Make a Tangram out of poster board (this is easy enough to cut with scissors). Or go the other way, and make one out of wood. Quarter-inch plywood or composition board works well. Be sure to sand any rough edges. Paint the wood (black looks nice) or seal it with varnish.

Some people say that long ago in China there lived a man named Tan who dropped a square tile on the floor. It broke into seven pieces. Try as he might, Tan was unable to put the pieces together again into a square. But he was able to fit them together in the shapes of birds, boats, and hundreds of other things! Do you suppose this is a true story?

GARDEN OF DELIGHTS

To an artist, an apple is more than something tasty to eat—
it's something beautiful to paint or to sculpt. Artists have
been inspired by plants and gardens for thousands of years.
Fruits, flowers, and vegetables are well represented in the art
world, from centuries-old mosaics of baskets brimming with
luscious edibles to modern botanical illustrations.

FOOLING MOTHER NATURE

You can't fool Mother Nature, as the saying goes, but you sure can try! Here are some ingenious flowers made from natural materials that you can "grow" right in your kitchen.

SEED FLOWERS

Seeds of all sorts, such as sunflower, squash, apple, pumpkin, and melon seeds (see *Note*)
Poster board scraps
Needle or awl
Florists' wire
Florists' tape
White glue

Note Save the seeds from fruits and vegetables that you eat. Wash the seeds thoroughly and let them dry. (This takes a few days, or you can speed things up by putting them in a 250°F oven for about an hour.) You can also use garden seeds that come in packets—perhaps some that you didn't get a chance to plant last season.

1. Cut a small circle the size of a quarter out of poster board for each flower. Poke two holes in the center of the circle with a needle or awl.

2. Cut a 12″ piece of florists' wire. Stick one end up through one hole and down through the other, twisting it around itself under the poster board circle. Wrap the wire with florists' tape.

3. Squirt some glue around the edge of the circle. Place a ring of seeds right around the circle, letting them hang over the edge slightly. Add some more glue and make a smaller ring of seeds, inside the first ring. Add another ring inside of that one. Place a single seed right in the middle if there's room.

4. Let dry completely. Spray with clear acrylic spray, if you like.

Tip Seeds come in a variety of shades of brown, but you can dye many seeds any color you like with fabric dyes or food colors. Mix some dye with a little water in a small jar, add the seeds, and let sit for a few hours. Drain the seeds and let them dry before using them.

Variations on a Theme
You can make other "flowers" from things you pick up on walks through the woods and meadows. Your garden may also yield some interesting finds.

Dried seed heads from poppies, black-eyed Susans, and teasels are very striking, even on their own. But if you wire some pine needles around the base of a

▶

Seeds come in all sorts of shapes and sizes. They can be as small as finely-ground pepper (many wildflower seeds are tiny) to as large as your fingernail (pumpkin and squash seeds are both quite large).

"Seed money" is an expression referring to money that is invested (planted) with the hope that it will grow!

teasel, you'll have a very unusual flower unlike any you've ever seen before!

Or attach a handful of seed cases from a luminaria (honesty) plant to the scales of a pine cone (rub the covering off the seed cases first).

A little spot of glue will hold them in place. Slip a wire through the base of the cone as a stem, and cover it with florists' tape.

What other fanciful flowers can you create from natural materials?

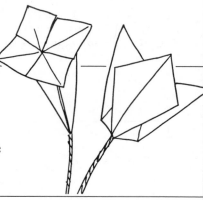

FLORAL FOLDS

Take a piece of paper, fold it this way and that, and presto—a paper flower that's almost as lovely as the real thing. You can make a whole bouquet using this Japanese paper-folding technique.

Did you know?
Tulips originated in the area of modern-day Turkey, Iran, and Afghanistan. Today all the tulip bulbs planted in this country come from Holland.

ORIGAMI TULIP

| 6″ origami paper (see *Note*) |
| Florists' wire |
| Florists' tape |
| White glue |

Note You can use any thin paper cut into squares to make origami flowers (and other figures). Gift wrapping paper is especially nice. Vary the size of the squares to make blooms of different sizes.

1. Place the paper colored-side down. Fold it in half to make a triangle.

2. Fold the right-hand point over to the left side, so that the top of this fold is parallel to the base of the triangle.

3. Fold the left-hand point over to the right side.

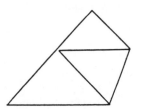

4. Unfold the paper back to the triangle. Slip your finger between the layers on the right, and push the folded part back into a kite shape.

Do the same on the other side.

Crease Line

5. Turn the paper over. Fold the edges in at the crease lines. The front and back should look exactly the same.

6. Fold in half. Fold up the bottom point (from the fold side). Crease very well.

Fold here

7. Open up the flower so that it looks like it did in step 5. Push the bottom diamond shape up inside the flower—reversing the creases. The flower will pop out to look like this.

Push this up

8. Cut a 12″ piece of florists' wire, bend down one end into a hook and poke it through the inside of the flower (from the top). Wrap florists' tape around the wire, starting up near the paper flower. Use a little glue to secure the tape to the flower and to hold the flower shut, if necessary.

ORIGAMI TRUMPET FLOWER
6″ origami paper
Florists' wire
Florists' tape
White glue

1. Place the paper colored-side up. Fold in half to make a rectangle.

Fold in half again to make a square.

2. Open up the paper (keep it colored-side up) and fold it in half to make a triangle.

Fold in half again to make a smaller triangle.

The Japanese learned how to fold paper from the Chinese, some time in the 6th century when the Chinese introduced paper to Japan. Despite this long history, the word *origami* is a recent one. From *oru,* "to fold," and *kami,* "paper," the word was coined in 1880 by a teacher at a Japanese kindergarten.

▶

Several flowers are trumpet-shaped, among them the bindweeds and the Morning Glory.

3. Push the top layer out and up and flatten it into a diamond shape.

Turn the paper over and do the same to the other side.

4. Fold the edges of the top layer in to meet at the center line.

Turn the paper over and do the same on the other side.

5. Fold the top down (all layers) about a third of the way from the top.

6. Unfold and push the petals down, flattening the two diamond shapes on either side into petals.

7. Cut a 12″ piece of florists' wire, bend one end into a hook and poke it through the inside of the flower (from the top). Wrap it with florists' tape, starting up near the flower. Use a little glue to secure the tape to the flower.

The Japanese are also well known for their distinctive arrangements of real flowers. *Ikebana* ("arrangement of living plant materials") is one style of flower arranging that is used to "illustrate" ideas with color and form, such as the seasons, or a feeling of quiet.

Look for some of the many books containing detailed instructions for origami objects. You'll find everything from seasonal decorations for all of our American holidays to traditional Japanese symbols, such as the crane, the best known Japanese symbol for good luck.

POINSETTIA

CRANE

PETAL PRESERVE

Flower blossoms and leaves can be given new life when they are pressed flat and dried. Here are two ideas for using those plants you pick on your walks to your garden, your windowbox, or through the wilds.

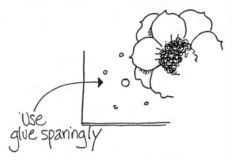

PRESSED FLOWER BOOKMARK

Flower blossoms, leaves, ferns, and grasses
Clean scrap paper
Fat book or plant press (see *Plant Press* on page 98 for one you can make)
Heavy paper, about 2½″ × 2½″ × 8″
Clear Contact® paper, enough to cover paper
X-acto knife

Note You can press just about any plant material that isn't too fat. Avoid garden blooms with very hard centers or those that have very fleshy petals.

1. The blossoms and leaves you press should be fresh and dry (wait until the afternoon to pick blooms if they're wet with dew). Sandwich the plants between sheets of clean paper. Place these between the pages of a thick book, or put them in between the layers of cardboard in your press.

Press the plants for 1–2 weeks, or until they are completely dry.

2. Lay all your pressed plant material out so that you can see what you have to work with. Handle the plants carefully as they are fragile. Try to plan an arrangement in your head, so that you can avoid moving the pressed plants around too much.

3. Glue the pressed flowers and leaves to the piece of heavy paper.

Use just a spot of glue for each. Let dry for a few minutes.

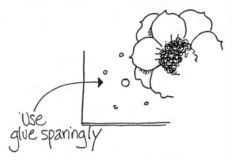

Use glue sparingly

4. Cover the entire bookmark with a piece of clear Contact® paper that is slightly larger than the bookmark. Lay it over the plants, starting at one end. Rub your fingers over the Contact® paper as you lower it to press out any air bubbles.

5. Trim the excess Contact® paper from the perimeter of the bookmark.

For a nice touch, punch a hole in one end of the bookmark and loop a piece of satin ribbon through it.

▶

You can use pressed flowers and other plant material to decorate candles. Glue the flowers directly on the candle with a little white glue; let dry completely. Coat the entire candle with slightly watered-down glue to protect the flowers.

Use pressed flowers to make a border for a favorite poem.

PRESSED FLOWER COLLAGE

Flower blossoms, leaves, ferns, and grasses
Fat book or plant press
Scissors
Thick cardboard, about 5″ × 7″
Frame with glass

Note Make your pressed flower collage in a standard size, such as 5″ × 7″, or 8″ × 10″. That way you can use a purchased frame that already has glass in it.

1. Press your flowers and leaves as described in *Pressed Flower Bookmark.* Lay them all out so you can see what you have to work with.

2. Make a pleasing arrangement of blossoms and leaves or use the plant material to create an imaginary scene such as the one shown here. Use the scissors to cut out

parts of leaves and thin bark to make the roof of the house. Snip stems into short lengths and lay them side by side to make the fence. The trees in this picture are the tops of ferns and other plants. Use a very small amount of glue to stick the plants to the cardboard.

Ferns make good "trees"

3. Place the cardboard in the frame. Hang the picture away from direct light. Sunlight quickly fades most dried flowers.

PLANT PRESS

In a pinch, you can always press blossoms and leaves between the pages of a fat book. But a plant press is an even better idea, and this simple press isn't hard to make.

You need two pieces of ¼″ plywood or masonite cut to size. A 6″ × 8″ rectangle is a good size for a portable press to take along with you on walks; make the press larger, if you like, if you plan to leave it at home.

Drill holes in the four corners of each board and attach them to one another with long bolts topped with wing nuts.

Make holes 1″ from edges

Cut several pieces of cardboard the size of your press. Trim a triangle off each corner where the bolts go.

Cut away all 4 corners

Tighten the nuts evenly at all four corners to put enough pressure on the plants to press them.

BE STILL

Vases full of flowers and bowls of fruit are often the subject of paintings known as still lifes. You can use these or some of your favorite belongings to create an artful composition.

STILL LIFE
Everyday objects of your choosing
Paper
Paints, markers, or colored pencils

1. Spend some time arranging the objects you have chosen, so that you're happy with the way they look. Play around with clustering the objects together or setting one apart from all the others.

Use a piece of cloth or a towel to cover a plain surface. Drape the fabric in interesting folds. Position a light to shine on your composition to highlight some of the objects and cast shadows on some of the others.

2. Lightly sketch in all the objects. Then make a finished drawing or painting, paying special attention to the shapes, textures, and colors. Add shading to make solid objects look three-dimensional. (See *Shipshape* on this page for hints on drawing three-dimensional objects.)

Tip If you can't complete your painting in one sitting, leave it and come back to it later. That's one of the nice things about a still life—it really does hold still!

SHIPSHAPE

There are four basic shapes that make up just about any object. If you practice drawing these shapes and learn to see how they are a part of everyday objects, drawing is a lot easier. Use a medium-soft pencil and plenty of inexpensive paper for practice drawing.

Start with the cube. A cube is nothing more than a box. It can be square or rectangular in shape. It also looks different depending on the angle from which it's viewed. Here's a tissue box seen straight on at eye level.

EYE LEVEL

▶

When the French painter, Paul Cézanne, painted people, he had them pose for long hours (because he was a slow and careful artist). If they moved, he would scold, "Sit like an apple!"—a subject he much preferred to paint. Cézanne painted over 200 still lifes during his lifetime.

Tricks of the Trade

There are many ways to create shading when drawing three-dimensional objects. Try crosshatching—making a series of lines that cross one another.

The more overlapping lines, the darker the area.

Experiment with stippling—creating different tones with tiny dots. Space them far apart for lighter tones; group them densely for darker areas.

Smudging, especially when drawing with a soft pencil, is another way to add shading.

SHIPSHAPE, CONTINUED

Here's what it looks like if you view it from above. Practice drawing a tissue box or a table from different angles.

The next shape is a sphere or round ball. A ball is easy to draw—just draw a circle! But an apple is also a sphere, and it's never perfectly round. You also have to remember that you want to give your apple the feeling of roundness, even though you are drawing it on a flat piece of paper. Look how just this one extra line makes the apple appear solid and round.

A cylinder is a sphere with straight sides. Take a drinking glass, for instance. Seen from the side, the sides of the glass are straight lines, but the top and bottom look like squashed ovals. (These are called ellipses.)

ELLIPSES

Practice drawing a glass or a flower pot (it, too, is a cylinder with sides that get narrower toward the bottom). The tops and bottoms of these cylinders look slightly different, depending on the angle that you are looking from.

Lastly, there is the cone. An

ice cream cone is a perfect example of a cone. Look at how the opening is an ellipsis when the cone is viewed lying down. Practice drawing the cone from different angles.

Now draw some objects that are made up of these different shapes. How about a glue bottle? It's a cylinder topped with a cone. A table lamp? This one is made up of several cylinders and spheres.

SQUARE ONE

Not all still lifes are painted, of course. Here's one that is made one square at a time, like a mosaic. You can create a dazzling still life with tiny colored paper "tiles."

PAPER MOSAIC

Colored paper in assorted colors
Ruler
X-acto knife
Scissors
White glue
Black paper, about 5″ × 7″
Clear varnish

Note The instructions here are for paper squares 1/4″ in size. You can use larger squares but you won't be able to get as much detail.

1. Cut the paper into 1/4″ squares. The quickest way to do this is to cut the paper in 1/4″-wide strips first, then snip the strips into squares.

To do this, gather up your paper into a stack. Mark a row of lines 1/4″ apart on the top sheet. Using a ruler to guide you, cut along each line with the X-acto knife.

Run the knife along each line several times to cut through the whole stack.

← 1/4″ APART

Gather together those strips that are the same color. Cut them into 1/4″ pieces with the scissors. Put each color in a separate bowl or pile.

2. Pencil the outline of your design on the black paper. Keep the design simple because it's hard to get a lot of detail with such a small mosaic.

3. Start by covering the outlines of your design with paper squares. Glue the squares down one by one, leaving a little space around each square. Here's a trick that makes handling the tiny squares easier. Squirt some glue on a scrap piece of paper. Dip just the tip of your finger into the glue. Place your glued finger on a square—it will lift right up. Use your other hand to flip the square over and position it on your paper.

Gluey finger will stick to squares

4. Now fill in the design, and the background. Follow the curves of your outline. Cut the squares into smaller pieces to fit into any tight, irregular spots.

The Story of Art
Mosaics originated in the Near East, where they were made as early as 3000 B.C. It was not until around 800 B.C. that they became very popular, especially as floor designs.

The first mosaics were made with rounded pebbles. Later, glass and colored marble chips were used. Still later, specially-made square tiles were made from clay, glazed in every color of the rainbow.

▶

Pick up some paint sample cards (look for these at a hardware store) and cut them into squares. These come in every color imaginable!

5. Brush or spray a couple of coats of clear varnish on the paper to protect the mosaic.

Tip To help your design really stand out, make sure there is plenty of contrast (light versus dark) in your mosaic. For instance, make the background squares much lighter (or darker, for a different effect) than those you choose to use in the design itself.

You can also use colored paper to create a more subtle mosaic. Cut plenty of paper in various shades of the main colors of your picture. Suggest the roundness of the forms in the mosaic by going from light to dark (the darker shades giving the appearance of shadow).

Mosaics were used to decorate churches until the 12th century when stained glass windows took their place.

TILE MOSAICS

Once you've mastered paper mosaics, you may want to go on to make mosaics using real tiles. You can purchase glass tiles made especially for mosaic work, or you can break old ceramic bathroom and kitchen tiles into little pieces (the shapes will be irregular, but that's okay). Place the tiles between some folded newspaper, and hit lightly with a hammer. Wear goggles to protect your eyes from flying pieces.

Make a frame out of plywood and pine molding. Glue or nail the molding around the perimeter.

Draw your design on the plywood. Glue the tile pieces in position with white glue. Leave a little space between each piece of tile. Let dry completely.

Mix some grout (this is available wherever tiles are sold) to a thick, creamy consistency. Spread it over the mosaic, forcing it down between all the tiles by pulling a piece of cardboard over the surface. Before the grout dries, scrape as much off the surface of the tiles as you can. Then run a damp sponge over the tiles and the molding to clean them. Let the grout dry.

Scrub any remaining grout off the mosaic. Sand any dried grout off the frame. You can hang this mosaic or use it as a trivet or table decoration.

A local building supplier may have some broken tiles you can have.

FRUTTI-TUTTI

With a little paper and paste, you can model a whole bowl of fruit that looks good enough to eat.

PAPIER-MÂCHÉ FRUIT

Newspaper
Tape
Paper towels
1/4 cup flour
Saucepan
Tissue paper in assorted colors
White glue
Medium-gauge wire, about 2' long
Florists' tape

Note The fruit shown here is covered with colored tissue paper, but you can also paint it, if you prefer.

1. Make some flour and water paste. Mix 1/4 cup flour with 4 cups water in a saucepan. Bring to a boil; cook until it is a smooth and creamy consistency. Set aside to cool.

2. Meanwhile, tear some of the newspaper into short strips (leave some of the sheets whole to form into the basic fruit shapes).

3. Crumple up half-sheets of newspaper to make the apples, oranges, and pears. These are basically round balls; make the pear's shape by taping a smaller ball on top of the larger one.

PEAR

Use a half-sheet to make a banana. Twist the newspaper into a curved crescent, taping it so the curve will hold its shape.

BANANA

Individual grapes are made from small pieces of paper rolled into balls.

GRAPES

4. Cover the basic fruit shapes with strips of newspaper moistened with the flour and water paste. Overlap the strips slightly. Make at least 3 layers of newspaper strips. For the best results, let each layer dry before adding another (this way there is less distortion). Use torn paper towels for the final layer. Take care to smooth out any wrinkles and lumps. Let dry for 3–5 days.

5. Choose tissue paper colors for each piece of fruit. Smear slightly watered-down white glue over the fruit shapes and cover them with tissue paper cut to size. Experiment with using different shades of one color to suggest natural coloring. Let dry completely.

Don't limit yourself to fruit. Papier-mâché eggplants, green peppers, and pea pods bursting with peas are lots of fun to make, too.

Did you know?
Tutti-frutti is Italian for "all fruits."

EDIBLE BLOOMS

Presenting food that not only tastes good but looks good, too, is truly an art. Chefs sometimes garnish dishes with flowers and fruit made from unexpected ingredients. You can add an artistic touch to your meals at home, too.

The Japanese are renowned for the visual artistry of their prepared foods. Much attention is paid to color, texture, and the way that foods are arranged on plates. The Japanese are particularly adept at creating unusual garnishes from common vegetables.

VEGETABLE & FRUIT GARNISHES

LONG–STEMMED RADISH ROSES

Red radishes, one per rose
Scallions, one per rose
Thin bamboo skewers, one per rose (see *Note*)
Green cabbage, one small head
Bowl

Note Look for bamboo skewers in the kitchenware section of department stores and supermarkets. They are usually sold in packages of 50 or 100.

1. Cut the root end off each radish. Make a series of vertical cuts in each all the way around. Be careful not to cut all the way through. Place the radishes in a bowl of cold water. Refrigerate overnight.

The next day, notice how the radishes have "bloomed" or opened up.

2. Cut the root end off each scallion. Insert a skewer in each scallion, pushing it up through one leafy tip (most scallions branch out into two or three leaves). Cut that leaf back just enough to expose the tip of the skewer.

3. Place an opened radish "bloom" on the tip of each scallion "stem." That completes one flower.

4. Slice the cabbage in half. Place it flat-side down inside a bowl. Stick the "long-stemmed roses" into the cabbage. Shred the remaining half of the cabbage (use a grater or a knife to cut thin slivers). Cover the upturned cabbage base with the shredded cabbage, to look like grass.

Tip For "roses" without stems, omit the scallions and skewers, and place the radishes directly on the serving platter.

CARROT CARNATIONS

Carrot
Vegetable peeler
Sharp knife
Toothpicks

1. Peel the carrot. Cut it into thin slices. Put all the slices in a bowl of cold water and refrigerate overnight.

2. Notice how the slices have curled and become twisted. Spear 3 to 5 slices on a toothpick to make a flower.

CITRUS WATERLILIES
Orange or grapefruit
Sharp knife
Green paper
Scissors

Note One piece of fruit makes two lilies.

1. Cut a zigzag pattern into the orange or grapefruit with the knife. Be sure to thrust the blade well into the fruit. Work your way around the entire fruit, ending right where you began.

Pull the two halves apart.

2. Cut some leaf shapes out of the green paper. Arrange the citrus "waterlilies" on top of the paper "pads."

MARZIPAN FLOWERS & FRUITS
Uncolored marzipan (look in the gourmet section of your market)
Food colors
Powdered sugar

Note Marzipan is a confection made from ground almonds, egg whites, and sugar. It is available in tube-shaped packages, the smallest weighing 7 ounces. It also comes pre-colored in kit form.

1. Divide the marzipan into sections, one for each color. (A little goes a long way, so use just half the tube for starters, if you like.) Add a few drops of food coloring to each piece of marzipan; leave one section uncolored. Green, yellow, red, and brown are just a few colors that work well for making fruit and flowers.

Work the food coloring into the marzipan with your fingers. Make sure the color is evenly distributed. If the marzipan seems sticky, knead in a little powdered sugar to firm it up.

2. Use the marzipan like modeling clay to create flowers and miniature fruit. Roll it between your fingers to make round shapes such as the apple, pear, and banana shown here. Use a tiny bit of brown for stems and the ends of the banana.

Flatten some marzipan on your work table (dust the surface with powdered sugar so that the marzipan won't stick to the table). With a small knife cut out shapes such as petals for the flower and leaves.

Use your marzipan flowers and fruit to decorate cakes, cupcakes, and cookies.

Marzipan can be used to create more than just fruit and flowers. Model little animals from the paste; roll it out and cut out letters from the alphabet to personalize a cake. Use your imagination to create some delicious decorations of your own.

LAY OF THE LAND

Many artists get their inspiration from nature. From the colors of a winter sunset to the trees that shade your street, there is untold beauty in the natural world.
Whether you live in the country or in the heart of a bustling city, just outside your front door is a landscape ready to inspire *you*. Gather up your gear and head outdoors!

ON A CLEAR DAY

Drawing and painting outdoors is a wonderful way to
get to know the world around you. Every season—even every day—
there's something new to observe.

LANDSCAPE

Paper, large sheets
Colored pencils, markers, or paint
Sturdy cardboard or masonite to put under the paper

Note You may not need a separate support for your paper, if your paper comes in a pad with a cardboard back.

1. Walk around until you find just where you want to view the landscape. Things look very different depending on your vantage point. An outdoor view seen from high up (from a second-story window or from the top of a small rise) is quite different when viewed from ground level.

Viewed from
ground level

Draw an imaginary frame around the part of the scene you want to paint. Choose something like a tall tree or a grouping of houses as a focal point.

2. With a pencil, lightly sketch in the main elements of your picture. Leave out anything that doesn't "belong"—anything that makes the picture confusing or that competes with the parts you want to stand out. You can do this because it is your drawing, and not a photograph.

Pay attention to perspective. See *Distant Relations* on page 108 for some perspective pointers.

3. Color the landscape. Make the background colors lighter than those in the foreground or front of the picture. This helps to give your drawing depth and makes it look more like a real landscape.

Painters who live in towns and cities sometimes paint "townscapes" and "cityscapes."

Artists in Japan and China were painting landscapes as long as 1,000 years ago. It was not until the mid-17th century, however, that artists in Europe thought to paint landscapes for their own sake.

Before this, landscapes were found only as backgrounds for paintings of other subjects. It was the Dutch who first took up landscape painting. They were interested in showing nature realistically and became very skilled at painting large areas of sky.

▶

The Story of Art
In the 1870s a group of French artists became interested in painting outdoors in natural sunlight. In order to capture the effect of the light before it changed, they painted quickly with loose brushstrokes. One of the painters, Claude Monet, exhibited a painting entitled *Impression: Sunrise.* From this painting's title came the name given to the style of painting these artists perfected—impressionism.

Did you know?
Trompe l'oeil (trawmp LOY) is French for "fool the eye."

DISTANT RELATIONS

There are a few tricks you can use to give your landscapes a feeling of depth and to make them more realistic looking. Draw objects and lines the way they appear rather than the way they really are.

Objects appear smaller the farther away they are. They also usually appear higher up the far-

ther away they get.

Parallel lines appear to be closer together as they get farther away. They look as if they come together at the horizon.

Objects in the foreground or front of a picture are more distinct and vivid than those objects in the background. Foreground objects are brighter in color; objects in the background are lighter and hazier looking.

FOOLED YOU!

Windows not only let in light but offer a glimpse of the world outside. Here's a way to make the view from a window anything you want!

TROMPE L'OEIL WINDOW

Sturdy cardboard, about 20″ × 30″
Colored pencils, markers, or paint
Yardstick or long ruler

Note This type of painting is especially effective painted directly on a wall. Check with your parents before you ever paint on walls, however. If you do intend painting it on a wall, it's a good idea to make a cardboard version first as a practice piece.

1. Draw the outlines of the window frame on the cardboard. Match the size and style of those windows near where you will hang the painting, or make the window any way you like.

Give the illusion of depth by drawing the bottom half of the window as it might look if viewed from above.

2. Pencil in the landscape or outdoor scene as it would be seen from the window. For fun, add an object sitting on the inside window sill, such as a potted plant.

3. Color in the painting. Paint the window frame with two shades of the same color. Use the darker shade to suggest shadows cast by the frame.

Make the outdoor scene lighter in color, so that it appears to be in the distance. Paint the object on the windowsill, paying special attention to how it would look lit with the bright light from the window.

4. Hang the picture, either level with the other windows in the room, or at a logical height.

Variations on a Theme
Paint a picture directly on an interior door. Paint a door slightly ajar, showing a glimpse of what is going on in the room beyond.

GLORIOUS GARDENS

With some printed and patterned paper, a pair of scissors, and glue, you can make a garden that's in bloom all year long.

CUT–PAPER COLLAGE

Sturdy cardboard, about 9″ × 12″
Assorted printed and plain papers, such as geometric and floral gift wrap, note cards, and wallpaper
Scissors
White glue

1. Cut out individual flowers and leaves from the printed paper you have collected. Cut your own flower shapes from the smaller over-all patterned paper. Cut stems, tree trunks, lawn, and sky from plain colored paper.

Have on hand various patterned and colored papers to add to your picture as you make it.

2. Plan your picture around the paper you have cut out. Play with color combinations and contrast (light versus dark) to make the most of the different scale patterns and prints. Don't glue anything down yet.

▶

The Hanging Gardens of Babylon were one of the seven wonders of the ancient world. According to legend, they were built by Nebuchadnezzar II (604–562 B.C.).

Artist's Profile
Claude Monet, a French painter living from 1840 to 1926, was an avid gardener. Many of his later works were inspired by the vast gardens at his home in Giverny. Monet painted 48 canvases of water lilies alone from 1904 to 1908. Some of these paintings are enormous. Up close all you see is thick paint and brushstrokes. Only when you stand well back can you make out the flowers themselves.

Some heavier colored-papers are made by printing the color onto white paper. When you tear one of these types of papers, the ragged edges show up white.

3. When you are happy with the picture you have made, glue the paper in place. Paste down the large areas first, such as the sky or the expanse of lawn.

SKY

GRASS

Cut them so they butt up to one another, or so they overlap slightly. Build up the picture by gluing down the flowers and foliage, and other elements, one by one.

Tip Brush on a coat of clear varnish or polymer medium, if you like, to protect the collage and give it a soft sheen.

Variations on a Theme
Use printed fabrics instead of paper for this collage. Use an iron-on bonding material such as Stitch Witchery® to adhere the fabric pieces to either a cardboard or fabric background.

Study a real garden to see how flowers are interplanted for effect. Some gardeners strive for harmony, planting flowers in one or two related colors. Other people prefer the more exciting look of flowers in complimentary colors planted next to one another.

SURF'S UP

A painting of the ocean and its shoreline is often called something other than a landscape. It's known as—you guessed it—a seascape. Here's an interesting way to capture the majesty of the sea on paper.

TISSUE PAPER SEASCAPE
White poster board, about 9″ × 12″
Colored tissue paper, in blues, blue-greens, and tans
White glue
Brush

Note If you don't have any white poster board on hand, glue a sheet of white paper onto any piece of sturdy cardboard.

1. Mix some white glue with a little water in a small bowl or glass.

2. Tear the tissue paper into irregular pieces. Brush some glue onto the poster board and place the paper over it, one piece at a time. Brush more glue over the paper to make it lay flat. Arrange the torn tissue pieces so that some overlap; leave some white space between some of the pieces to suggest waves.

3. Add some land (perhaps an island in the distance), if you like, and some sky. Let dry completely. Trim the ragged edges of the picture with a pair of scissors or an X-acto knife.

Trim all sides

Tip Tissue paper "bleeds" when it gets wet. Take advantage of this for some interesting effects. Glue a piece of tissue paper down; lift it off before the glue dries. Some of the dye is left behind. Notice how the glue becomes slightly tinted. Use it to paint with, like watercolors, wherever you want some subtle color.

Colored tissue paper is also perfect for more abstract collages. Overlap two colors to create a third color.

Winslow Homer, an American artist living from 1836 to 1910, is best known for his coastal and country scenes. He once said, "Never put more than two waves in a picture: it's fussy."

LIGHT OF THE MOON

Just imagine what things would look like if colors were as bright at night as they are by day. Do you suppose this is what you'd see on a walk through the jungle on a moonlit night?

WAX RESIST NIGHTSCAPE

Medium-weight paper, about 9″ × 12″
Crayons in assorted colors
Black poster paint or watercolor
Large brush

Note Fluorescent crayons work especially well with this technique.

1. Draw a picture of the outdoors using crayons. Draw the jungle scene shown here or make up one of your own. Press down hard as you outline and color in the picture. Use plenty of bright colors (and white, too) for the best effect.

2. Brush the poster paint over the entire drawing. The wax in the crayons "resists" the paint, making the drawing show up clearly against the black background. Let dry.

Variations on a Theme
Make this drawing using what's known as a scratchboard technique. Cover the entire surface of a piece of paper with areas of solid color using different colored crayons. Press down hard on the crayons. Now cover all these colors with a thick layer of black crayon.

One of the best known night landscapes is Vincent Van Gogh's *The Starry Night*. Instead of pinpoints of light in a dark sky, Van Gogh's stars are huge, swirling orbs of light.

▶

Because oil pastels smudge easily, it's a good idea to protect pastel drawings with a spray fixative.

Scratch through the top layer of black with an instrument such as a pencil point, nail, or screwdriver. The colors underneath will appear as you draw the picture.

PASTEL PASTIMES

You're probably very familiar with crayons, but there's a similar drawing medium you might like to try that offers even more possibilities. Oil pastels (you may find these under the name Cray-pas®, a brand that takes its name from *cray*ons plus *pas*tels) are even brighter than crayons and are softer and easier to use.

Like crayons, oil pastels can be used with light or heavy pressure. Because they are so soft, however, they can be blended with your fingertip. When they are layed down thickly, they cover the paper completely.

Oil pastels can be thinned with turpentine or mineral spirits to create watercolor-like effects, too. Try dipping a cotton swab in turpentine and rubbing it on parts of an oil pastel drawing. Those parts will be lighter in color, and a little hazier looking, perfect for the backgrounds in landscapes, for instance.

A SAMPLING OF STARS

One star, our sun, dominates the landscape each day, but millions of distant stars bring the night sky to life. Here are two stars you can make. The first is a five-pointed star cut from a folded sheet of paper; the second is an eight-pointed version made from long, narrow strips of paper.

Stars have been depicted throughout history with three, four, five, six, seven, and even eight points!

FIVE-POINTED CUT STAR

Lightweight paper, 8½" × 11"
Scissors

1. Fold the paper in half crosswise. With the fold at the bottom, bring the lower right-hand corner up to the halfway point on the left side. Crease well.

2. Fold the right-hand edge over to the left and crease. Fold the remaining section on the left over to the right and crease.

3. Cut along the imaginary line indicated by the row of dots. The smaller portion is the star. Unfold it and see!

Tip Before you unfold the star, snip little bits out with the scissors. Your star will have an intricate lacy pattern just like snowflakes cut from paper.

EIGHT–POINTED WOVEN STAR

4 strips medium-weight paper, 3/4″ × 24″
Scissors
Thread or thin string
Needle

Note Three-quarter inch strips make a star that is 3¼″ across. Use thinner strips for a smaller star; wider ones for a larger star.

1. Fold each strip in half and cut the ends at an angle.

2. Weave the 4 strips together as shown. Pull the strips so they are snug.

3. Bend one of the top left-hand strips down. Bend one of the strips on the left over to the right. Bend one of the bottom strips up. Bend one of the right-hand strips over to the left, weaving it under the first strip to hold them all in place.

There are now 8 strips radiating from the central square. They are marked 1 through 8 in the drawing above to make the next steps clearer.

4. Fold strip 1 down at an angle as shown. Wrap the strip around to the back, bringing it to the front again and inserting it under the woven strip below it.

Pull the strip carefully, as far as it will go. A triangular point will form. Trim the strip flush with the woven section of the star.

5. Do the same with strips 7, 5, and 3, in that order. Trim the excess off each.

6. Turn the star over. Fold and tuck strips 8, 6, 4, and 2 (in that order), the same way you did the first four strips.

7. Poke a small hole in the star with a needle. Thread a piece of string through the hole and tie.

Variations on a Theme
Use two colors for a checker-board look (be sure to alternate them in step 2 of the instructions). Weave together four different colors for a very festive star.

Star light, star bright,
First star I see tonight:
I wish I may, I wish I might,
Have the wish I wish tonight.

Many national flags have stars on them. The flag of the United States has fifty which represent the fifty states. What other countries have stars on their flags? Are they all five-pointed?

Terraria were all the rage in the 19th century when Victorian households were not considered complete without a glass case planted with ferns.

The first botanical garden in Europe was founded in Padua, Italy in 1545.

PLANT PARADISE

You can create your own landscape indoors with living plants. Make a terrarium out of an old aquarium or glass bottle for a landscape that will practically take care of itself.

TERRARIUM

Glass aquarium, at least 10-gallon size
Gravel
Charcoal
Potting soil
Humidity-loving plants, such as ferns, mosses, and small flowering species like miniature African violets
Mister

Note Your local garden center will have everything you need for your terrarium (except the container).

1. Wash the aquarium with soap and water; rinse well. Place a ½″ layer of gravel on the bottom of the aquarium. On top of this sprinkle a layer of charcoal. Put about 2″ of damp potting soil over this.

POTTING SOIL

CHARCOAL

GRAVEL

2. Remove each plant from its pot by holding it upside-down in one hand and giving the pot a sharp tap. The plant should fall right out into your hand.

3. Make a shallow depression for each plant in the potting soil. Place each plant in position, spreading its roots out horizontally and packing potting soil around it. (This helps to slow the growth of the plants somewhat.) Arrange the plants so that there is a focal point (a tall plant) and an interesting mix of colors and textures, just as you would if you were planning a drawing.

FOCAL POINT

4. Spray the plants with the mister. Cover the top of the aquarium with a sheet of glass or with foil. Place the terrarium in indirect light, away from a heater.

Tip Terraria thrive with minimal care. Remove the lid for a short time if condensation collects on the inside of the glass; sponge away any algae that forms. Remove any dead leaves and blossoms, and trim those plants that are growing fast.

Variations on a Theme
For a different type of indoor landscape, plant a desert garden. Cacti and succulents can be grown together in a shallow container, even one without drainage holes. Put down a layer of gravel followed by a two-to-one mix of potting soil and sand.

Wear thick gloves when you transplant the cacti, or wrap a strip of folded newspaper around the plants to protect your hands from the sharp spines.

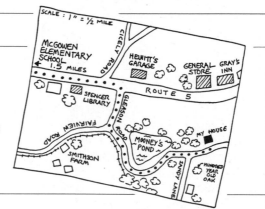

X MARKS THE SPOT

If you wanted to tell someone the way to your house, say, from your school, how would you go about it? You could give verbal directions, or you could make a map. This is a great way to get to know your neighborhood.

BIRDS' EYE VIEW MAP

Lightweight paper, about 12″ × 18″
Fine-point markers or colored pencils
Compass (optional)
Pedometer (optional)

Note You may already have a map of your general area, such as a topographical map or a map put out by your town or city. Use it to help you orient yourself, if you like.

1. Decide on the area you want to map. The map shown here is part of a rural school bus route, but you can make your map of your backyard, a nearby park, or anywhere you like.

2. To make your map as accurate as possible, measure the distance between major landmarks, such as turn-offs, crossroads and easy-to-identify buildings. If you are mapping a small area, walk the route, orienting yourself with a compass and counting your strides. (Or use a pedometer, a device that measures walking distances.)

BACKYARD MAP

If you are mapping a large area, ask your parents to drive the route with you. Use the odometer in the car (stopping frequently to make readings) to measure distances between landmarks.

Sketch a rough map of your route, penciling in all pertinent information.

3. Decide on the scale of your final map. The map shown here is drawn on the scale of 1″ to one-half mile. For mapping a backyard, a scale of 1″ to 1 yard (3 feet) might be a good choice. Be sure to indicate the scale and any other

features that you are showing with symbols in a legend or key.

SCALE: 1″ = 1 yd. (3 feet)
🌳 = tree
├──┤ = fence
〰️ = water
☐ = dwelling
▨ = business

4. Draw the final map. Color it with felt-tip markers or colored pencils. Add as much detail as you like. Let dry, then fold for easier carrying (see page 116 for a first-rate way to fold maps).

Tip Give your map a protective coating of spray varnish. Have an adult help you with this and be sure to do the spraying outdoors.

The United States Geological Survey was organized in 1879 for the purpose of making large-scale topographical maps.

The Story of Art
The oldest known map dates from 2300 B.C. It's a small Babylonian clay tablet showing a wealthy estate.

The oldest known folded map is an ancient Egyptian map drawn on papyrus. Its grid of creases indicates that it was folded much the way maps continue to be folded to this day.

▶

The study of maps and mapmaking is called cartography.

The maps used by pilots and sea captains are known as charts.

FOLDING A MAP

In order to fit in a pocket or the glove compartment of your car, most maps are folded. There are lots of ways of doing this, but none so as ingenious as this unusual method. Practice on a spare piece of paper before you fold your map in this way.

Start with a rectangle of paper. Fold the paper in half from the top to the bottom.

Fold the two top corners down so they meet in the middle. Crease well.

Return the corners to their original positions. Slip your fingers between the layers of the left side and push in and over so the paper is now folded as shown.

Turn the paper over and do the same on the back. The paper looks like this.

Push the top layer of the bottom left-hand corner in so that it overlaps the center slightly and looks like this.

Do the same on the right-hand side of the top layer.

Turn the paper over and repeat these last two overlapping folds. The map should look like this. Crease all the folds well with your fingernails.

To open the map, slip one thumb under the uppermost fold; slip the other thumb under the fold at the back. Pull apart and the map will magically open.

Maps can be made to show a variety of information. General reference maps are used to indicate the lay of the land, as well as roads and political boundaries such as states and countries.

Thematic maps are used to emphasize a topic or theme such as rainfall, population density, or natural resources.

HOME, SWEET HOME

As the saying goes, "Home is where you hang your hat"—or your baseball mitt or your ballet slippers! People throughout the world live in all sorts of houses. From grass huts to high-rise apartment houses, buildings for living in and for working in are designed with native materials, climate, and population density in mind.

Building styles are constantly evolving as fashions and customs change. Some buildings are always "in style" in their particular locale. What type of house do you live in?

NESTING INSTINCT

For a bird, home is where you build your nest. Many birds are finding it harder each year to find good nesting spots. You can help our fine-feathered friends make themselves at home with a sturdily-built birdhouse.

Supply the birds in your area with some nesting materials. Fill a mesh bag (the kind that onions come in) with short lengths of yarn and string, dried grass, even stuffing from old furniture and hair from a hairbrush. Hang the bag where the birds can find it, and watch them helping themselves to these materials.

WOODEN BIRDHOUSE

1″ × 6″ pine, 5 feet long
Pencil
Ruler
Screws or galvanized nails, about 2 dozen
2″ hinge
Saw
Drill, with ¼″ and 1½″ bits
Screwdriver or hammer

1. With a pencil and a ruler, mark the length of pine following the diagram shown here.

Another way to help out birds is to feed them in winter. Make a flat feeding table from some wood scraps, or fashion your own feeder from an empty milk carton or coffee can.

2. Cut the wood into six pieces. Make the cut separating the top and front pieces at an angle, as shown.

Angle this cut

3. Drill a ¼″ hole near the top of the back piece for hanging. Drill 5 or 6 ¼″ holes in the bottom piece for drainage. Drill a 1½″ hole in the center of the front piece, about 1½″ from the top.

4. Screw or nail the front and two sides to the bottom. Screw the back in place, positioning it so that it hangs a couple of inches below the house base. Lay the top in place; attach it to the back with the hinge.

5. Hang the birdhouse away from direct sun and out of reach of cats. It should be 5–10 feet off the ground. Many birds prefer to make their nests in dead trees, so hang the house away from dense shade.

ENTRANCE HOLE SIZES

This basic birdhouse appeals to a number of birds, but you can encourage certain species to nest in the house by changing the size of the entrance hole.

Bluebirds prefer the 1½″ opening called for in the instructions. Make the opening a little smaller for titmice and downy woodpeckers, say 1¼″ in diameter. Chickadees and house wrens like an even smaller hole—1⅛″ will do nicely for them.

IF I HAD A HAMMER

You don't need many tools to get started in woodworking. You can get by with just a saw (a good choice is a compass or keyhole saw which is easier to handle than a crosscut or ripping saw), a claw hammer (look for a lightweight adult model) and a supply of nails.

There are certain times, however, when you'll want to hold wood together with screws.

Match the screwdriver to the type of screw (Phillips-head or regular). It's a lot easier to screw in a screw, if you first make a pilot hole. Bang a nail partly in and pull it out, or drill a hole with a slightly smaller bit.

It's also a lot easier, and safer, to have something to hold your wood while you're working on it. A vice is like a second pair of hands, and strong ones at that!

There are both portable vices and those that clamp to worktables.

The earliest tool was probably the axe, made of flint or stone in Neolithic times (4000–5000 B.C.).

BUG BUNGALOW

Many insects make interesting guests in your home, especially when you provide them with comfortable lodgings. Here's a roomy cage you can make from a few things you may already have on hand.

INSECT CAGE

| Round cake pans, 2 the same size |
| Metal screen, about 12″ × 30″ |
| Masking tape |
| Non-hardening modeling clay |

Note You can also use pie plates for the top and bottom of this cage.

1. Cut the screen 12″ wide and a couple of inches longer than the circumference of the cake pans. (The circumference is the measurement around the outside or perimeter.)

2. Roll the screen into a tube that fits snugly into the cake pans. Tape the seam with the masking tape. Cover any raw edges with tape, too.

Many nature centers and museums have insect zoos. Look for one near you. If you have any questions regarding the care and feeding of insects, one of the zoo's staff will be happy to help you.

▶

Your house is probably already home to a number of insects. Flies spend the winter in a dormant stage inside many homes. Spiders live year-round high up in the corners of rooms (you've probably seen their webs). All sorts of other creatures make themselves at home in wooden furniture, rugs, and woolen sweaters!

3. Press some modeling clay along the inside perimeter of one of the pans. Place the screen tube in the pan. Pinch the clay all around the screen to secure it. Place the other pan on top of the screen.

Tip Provide food and water for any long-term insect residents. Put a sprig of the plant you found the insect on in a glass of water to keep it fresh. (Be sure to cover the glass with a piece of foil so that the insect doesn't drown). Sprinkle a few drops of water on a cotton ball to quench your insect's thirst. Don't forget to let

your guest go when you have finished watching it.

The first coins were issued around 700 B.C. in Lydia, an ancient country bordering on the Aegean. They were made from electrum (a gold and silver alloy) and had a picture of a tortoise on them.

CARDBOARD BOX BANK
Poster board, about 12″ × 28″
Medium-weight paper, about 3″ square
Ruler
X-acto knife
White glue
Paint

Note The bank shown here is about 5″ square by 6″ high.

SAVINGS INSTITUTION

The bank is the safest place to keep your money, but here's a good place for all your loose change until you make a deposit.

1. Draw the cutting outline of the bank on a piece of poster board. Use the dimensions shown here, or change them to suit the building you have in mind.

Be sure to mark the dotted fold lines.

2. Cut out the bank and its roof with either scissors or the X-acto knife. Score along the dotted lines by cutting only part way through the cardboard with the knife. Cut out the coin slot in the roof and the circle in the base of the bank.

3. Paint the cardboard. This is easiest to do before the bank is assembled. Let dry completely. Glue a circle of paper over the access hole in the base of the bank.

BOTTOM OF BANK

4. Fold the cardboard along the scored lines. Glue the tabs to the inside walls so they don't show. Glue one at a time; hold the joint together for a minute or so until the glue bonds. Attach the roof to the four gable tabs.

5. To remove money from the bank, tear off the paper covering the hole in the base. Glue a new piece of paper back on when you want to fill the bank again.

Variations on a Theme

Use your imagination, and any materials at hand, to create your own architectural bank. Give your bank a flat roof or a gambreled roof (the kind you see on a lot of barns). Make a pyramid from cut and scored corrugated cardboard. Use an empty oatmeal box to make a tower bank. Make it a free-standing tower or part of a building. Make a whole castle to hold the royal coffers!

A penny saved is a penny earned.
Poor Richard's Almanac

DELICIOUS DWELLING

Here's an edible cookie house that's made up of all sorts of goodies that are good for you. Be sure to take a photograph of your house, because it's guaranteed not to last long!

COOKIE HOUSE

Peanut butter sugar wafers, 12 per house
Graham crackers, 3 per house
Royal icing (recipe on page 122)
Assorted nuts and dried fruits

Shredded wheat cereal, 1 large piece
Sturdy cardboard, about 8″ square

1. Make four walls for the house from three peanut butter wafers placed horizontally. Hold them together with some icing piped along the edges. Join the four walls at the corners with more icing.

Some real houses have ornately carved wooden decorations along the edges of their roofs and porches. This is sometimes known as gingerbread style!

▶

Remember Hansel and Gretel? It seems they may have been responsible for the birth of the gingerbread house. In the 1800s, the Brothers Grimm told the tale of two children who happen upon a wicked witch living in a gingerbread house. The story was turned into a popular opera by Engelbert Humperdinck, and everyone who saw it wanted to make a gingerbread house of their own.

2. Cut a graham cracker in half diagonally for the gables. Pipe some icing along two ends of the house; attach the gables. Pipe icing along the gables and place two double graham crackers on them to form a peaked roof.

Place the house on the cardboard and set aside to dry.

3. Decorate the house and yard. The house shown here has a shingled roof made from whole almonds stuck on with just a little bit of icing. The door and windows are made from strips of dried apricot "glued" in place with icing. Raisins are used for the door handle and to line the path up to the front door. The grass is shredded wheat sprinkled over some piped icing that has been spread about with a knife. Decorate your house any way you like.

Variations on a Theme

To make a larger dwelling, make a batch of gingerbread cookie dough. Roll it out and cut it into the walls and roof of a house. Look for a gingerbread recipe in a cookie cookbook or in an all-round basic cookbook.

You can decorate your house with candy, too, of course.

ROYAL ICING

Royal icing is perfect for decorating cookies and assembling cookie houses, because it dries hard. The following recipe makes about 2 cups, which is plenty for decorating 3 or 4 peanut butter wafer houses.

Combine 1½ cups sifted powdered sugar, 1 egg white, a pinch of salt, and 1 teaspoon lemon juice in a medium-size bowl. Beat with an electric mixer for at least 5 minutes, until the mixture is fluffy and stands in peaks when you lift out the beaters. Add more lemon juice if it seems too thick; more powdered sugar if it's too runny.

The easiest way to decorate with royal icing is to pipe it out

Royal icing can be tinted with food colors. Add more powdered sugar, if the food coloring makes the icing too thin.

of a decorating bag. If you have one, use it with a small plain tip. Otherwise, make your own from a heavy plastic bag. Fill the bag with about half the icing, squeezing it so it flows down into one corner. Cut the very tip of that corner with scissors. Twist the bag closed, squeezing the icing out with one hand while guiding it with the other hand.

Use royal icing to decorate cookies and cakes any time of year. With a fine "writing" tip, you can personalize confections, as well as draw designs and pictures on rolled cookies and cake tops.

CITY LIMITS

Want to be a town planner? With a bagful of wood scraps, you can build a whole town of houses and shops the scale of miniature cars and trucks. They are perfect for playing with both indoors and out.

SCRAP WOOD TOWN

Assorted wood scraps (see *Note*)
Saw
Sandpaper
Waterproof glue
Permanent markers or paint

Note You should be able to round up all sorts of interesting wood scraps. Ask a local carpenter for the scraps that accumulate at the end of a work day. Look for molding at a lumberyard. Check under

Settlements of houses and other buildings go by different names depending on how many people the settlement supports. Village, town, city, and metropolis are just some of the names used. What other ones can you think of?

Wood Products in the Yellow Pages. You can often purchase whole bags of turned wood scraps from the businesses listed.

1. Study the wood pieces you have collected. Some of the shapes may already look like buildings (or parts of buildings).

2. Glue the wood pieces with waterproof glue. (If you plan to play with the town indoors only, you can use white glue.) Let dry.

3. Paint the houses and shops, if you like. Add details with the permanent markers.

Variations on a Theme
Larger buildings can be made from cardboard cartons and other containers. Cut out windows and doors with scissors or an X-acto knife. Paint the boxes with thick poster paints or cover them with construction paper.

Some cities are built in a regular grid with streets crossing one another at right angles. Much of New York City is arranged in this way. Other cities have evolved along different lines. Paris is one city that has avenues radiating from a central point.

The city

St. Augustine, Florida is the oldest city in the United States. It was settled by the Spanish in 1565.

A HOME A-FLOAT

Not everyone lives in a house built on solid ground. Millions of people worldwide make their homes on the water. Here's a miniature houseboat you can make that is paddle-powered.

In Europe, canals were once used for transporting goods. There was room on the barges not only for the boatman, but for his whole family as well. Today many of these boats are used as vacation homes.

WOODEN PADDLEBOAT
1″ × 6″ pine, about 12″ long
1/4″ × 2″ pine, about 6″ long (see *Note*)
Saw
3 small nails
Hammer
Rubber band
String
Assorted wood scraps (optional)

Note Look for pine molding at a lumberyard that is close to 1/4″ × 2″ in size, or slice a thin piece from a larger board to these dimensions.

1. Draw the outline of a boat on the 1″ × 6″ pine, as shown. Cut the shape out with the saw.

2. Cut the 1/4″ × 2″ pine into two pieces about 3″ long. Carefully cut a notch in the middle of each piece, about halfway through, as shown.

Fit the two pieces together to make a cross. This is the paddle wheel.

3. Hammer two small nails on either side of the opening at the back of the boat. They should stick up about 1/2″ or so. Wrap the rubber band around the paddle (so that it straddles it) and hook the ends of the rubber band over the two nails.

4. Hammer the third nail to the front of the boat, again leaving the nail sticking up about 1/2″.

Tie a length of string to this nail (this is so you can easily retrieve the boat if it floats far from shore).

5. Use the assorted wood scraps to give the boat a little cabin, if you like. Another option is to simply string a railing around the perimeter of the boat.

6. To make the paddleboat go, simply wind up the rubber band nice and tight and release the boat in water.

In many harbors in Southeast Asia, thousands of houseboats are anchored next to one another. Families cook, eat, and sleep on their boats.

THE PLAY'S THE THING

With this simple wooden set-up and a few blankets or pieces of fabric, you can create a house, a shop, a puppet theater, or even a secret hiding place! Make the three frames as shown, or add on more for even larger structures.

WOODEN PLAY FRAMES

36 feet of 1″ × 1″ pine
12 L-shaped corner braces (with screws)
Saw
Drill, with ¼″ bit
Screwdriver
Sandpaper
3 leather strips, each 12″ long

Note If you can't find 1″ × 1″ lumber, have a lumberyard rip 1″ × 3″ pine boards down the middle.

1. Cut the lumber into six pieces 36″ long, and six pieces 32½″ long. Sand any rough spots off the ends of each piece.

2. Make a square with two 36″ pieces and two 32½″ pieces, as shown. Screw the wood together at the corners with the braces. Drill pilot holes first with the drill; then screw in the screws.

Make two more frames the same way with the remaining lumber.

3. Drill a ¼″ hole in the very center of each vertical side of each frame. Lace a leather strip through the holes of two frames to hold them together (lace them loose enough so the frames can be placed at right angles to one another).

To make a square house, lace the three frames together (the fourth side of the house is left open). To make a triangular structure, lace all three frames together. Remove one of the frames when you want to use the set-up as a partition in front of a doorway, for instance.

Tip Use sheets and lightweight blankets to drape over the frames to create houses and other play places. Place one or two frames in front of a doorway or other opening to make a puppet theater. Lash branches that have leaves on them to the frames to create a blind from which to watch wildlife.

There are other play structures you can make. Do you have a low-branching tree on your property? Make a tree house! If you'd rather keep your feet on the ground, use brush and fallen branches to construct a secret hide-away. Don't let winter and heavy snowfall keep you from enjoying house-building. Build a snow fort or an igloo using a bread pan to mold the snow into stackable bricks.

FINE FURNISHINGS

Since the beginning of time, people have taken pride in their surroundings. Comfort and utility always come first, but most home furnishings are decorated with meaningful and imaginative designs.

Potters, tinsmiths, basketmakers, and weavers are sometimes considered artisans rather than artists, but there's no question *artistry* plays a very important part in the making of household goods and furnishings.

A BANNER YEAR

Flags and banners are used to represent nations, communicate information, and add decoration. Design your own banner to hang in your room. Make it purely decorative or include some of your interests in the design to make it more meaningful.

FELT BANNER

Felt or burlap for the background, about 24″ × 36″
Felt squares in assorted colors
Fabric trims, such as rick rack, lace, braid, sequins, beads, and buttons
White glue
Needle and thread

Note Felt is the perfect choice for both a banner background and its decorative elements, because it doesn't ravel and can be glued. It also comes in a rainbow of colors. There are plenty of other fabrics you can use, however, but you should turn under any raw edges to prevent raveling.

1. Think about what you want to include in your banner. Sketch your ideas in color. Make a scaled-down version on graph paper, or cut out full-size pieces of paper colored with crayons or markers.

Then, pin them on the fabric to see how size, placement, and color work together.

GRAPH PAPER

2. Cut and assemble your banner, either gluing the pieces to the background or sewing them on. Use as little glue as possible, placing a series of dots over the back of each piece. Press glued pieces under weights such as a pile of books or bricks, until dry.

3. Hang the banner. You can do this in a number of ways. Simply tack it to a wall (or door) with pushpins or thumbtacks. For something a little fancier, fold over the top edge of the banner (you should have included a little extra in the length to do this) and glue or stitch a long pocket. Slip a

dowel or section of a broom handle through the pocket. Tie some cord to either end of the dowel and hang.

Variations on a Theme
The banner described above is best hung indoors or in a well-protected spot. To make a banner that is meant to hang outdoors, it's best to use fabrics that will stand up to the weather. Nylon is a good choice, as it dries quickly (so it won't mildew), but sturdy cotton and cotton blends, sprayed with a protective coating used on upholstery fabrics, work well, too. To make a Japanese carp windsock that is hung like a banner, see page 58.

You may have heard the story about Betsy Ross, and how she made the first flag for the United States. There is no historical evidence that she really did so. The first public mention of the fact was made by her grandson almost one hundred years later. He had no proof, unfortunately.

Did you know?
The word *banner* means "distinguished from others, especially in excellence." So that means a banner year is a very good year indeed!

THE MAGIC CARPET

Rugs and carpets are popular floor coverings because they are warm, muffle sound, and add color to a room. Here's a painted floorcloth you can make that has one other purpose— you can play checkers on it!

The Story of Art
Floorcloths were popular in both Europe and the United States during the 18th and 19th centuries. They were used not only as a way to duplicate extensive rugs, but they were popular as warm weather rugs, when the woolen ones were put in storage for the summer.

CHECKERBOARD FLOORCLOTH

1 yard 36"-wide canvas
Gesso (optional)
Ruler
Masking tape
X-acto knife
Latex housepaint or acrylic paints, in at least 2 colors
Brush
Polyurethane
White glue

Note There are many grades of canvas available. Artists' canvas made from linen or cotton fibers is very expensive. Look for a thinner canvas at your local fabric store. It is reasonably priced and works just as well.

1. Iron the canvas to smooth out any wrinkles. Find a place to lay it out flat, where it won't be disturbed. Place it on a layer of newspaper to protect the floor or work table.

2. Paint the canvas with gesso (an acrylic medium that is meant to be used under acrylic paints to make them brighter and hold up longer) or a coat of latex housepaint. If you are using housepaint, make it the lighter of the two colors you have chosen for your checkerboard pattern. Let dry.

3. Mark off the checkerboard grid with a ruler and pencil. A 36"-square piece of canvas can be marked off into 4" squares. (There are 64 squares in a checkerboard— 8 going one way, and 8 the other.)

Each square 4" x 4"

4. Carefully lay down strips of masking tape to mask off those squares that aren't painted the second color. Use the X-acto knife to trim the ends of the masking tape precisely. Use just enough pressure to cut through the tape, and not into the canvas. Press down hard on the tape to make sure the bond is good.

Mask around squares to be painted →

5. Paint the squares you have masked around with the second color. Work from the outside in to avoid getting paint under the tape. Let dry.

6. Peel away the masking tape. Place more tape along the outside edge of the checkerboard, and again about an inch from that, to mask off a border to be painted in the second color (or a third).

Paint the border; let dry. Remove the tape.

7. Turn the hem of the cloth under all the way around. Glue it in place. Put weights around the hem, such as books or bricks, until it dries.

Turn under hem

8. Paint one or two coats of clear polyurethane on the cloth to protect it from wear. (This is best done outdoors where there is plenty of ventilation. Ask your parents to help you with this step.) Let the first coat dry; then lightly sand it with fine sandpaper before painting on the second coat.

PLAY PIECES

You can use the checkers that come with a regular checkerboard to play the game on your floorcloth, but if you'd like the checkers bigger, here's a simple idea for making your own.

Cut 24 2½″ circles out of cardboard. Paint the fronts and backs of 12 of them in one color; paint the remaining 12 with another color (use the same colors you painted the checkerboard with or choose 2 different colors). On the backs of all 24 checkers, paint or draw a crown. When a piece is "kinged," simply turn the checker over to display the crown.

Variations on a Theme
Instead of painting a checkerboard pattern on a floorcloth, paint a design typical of other types of rugs. Paint the canvas in the earth colors of Navajo rugs (see *Mr. Sandman* on page 70 for some Indian motifs you can use). Create an intricate Oriental design or an abstract design typical of a Swedish rya rug. Copy a design from a book or from a rug in your house.

Checkers is an ancient game. It was popular in China, Java, and Borneo for hundreds of years before it made its way to Europe, and later the United States.

BOWLED OVER

You can make a very sturdy bowl with papier-mâché pulp and an open mold such as a colander or shallow bowl. Add decorative touches by modeling the pulp with your fingers or with paint.

PAPIER–MÂCHÉ PULP BOWL

Papier-mâché pulp (see page 74)

Mold, such as a colander or shallow bowl
Petroleum jelly

1. Have the papier-mâché pulp ready. Smear petroleum jelly on the inside of the colander or bowl you are using as a mold.

▶

The first pottery bowls were probably made by accident. Archaeologists speculate that clay was originally used to line woven baskets to make them watertight. It wasn't long before someone ventured to make a vessel just out of clay itself.

2. Press the pulp into the mold, patting it with your hands or the back of a wooden spoon to make a compact, even layer. Make sure the pulp is not too wet; squeeze out some of the moisture first to help speed up the drying.

Bring the pulp right up to the top of the mold and flatten it or taper the pulp at the top for a different look. You can also add a decorative rim to your bowl, by pinching the pulp with your fingers or pressing down on it with the tines of a fork (like a piecrust is decorated).

"PIE CRUST" RIM

3. Let the pulp dry. This takes from 4 to 7 days, depending on how warm it is. Slow drying is necessary to keep the pulp from drying unevenly and distorting.

4. Remove the bowl from the mold. (Insert a knife blade under the rim to ease it away from the mold.) Paint the bowl with acrylics, if you like, or cover it completely with a coat of clear varnish.

Variations on a Theme
Instead of using the inside of a bowl as a mold, invert the bowl and pat the pulp in place on the *outside* of a bowl. Be sure to coat the mold with petroleum jelly first. This gives your papier-mâché bowl a smooth finish on the inside and a rough one on the outside.

The earliest surviving objects made from papier-mâché are two Chinese helmets dating from the 2nd century. They were painted with many coats of lacquer which served to strengthen the helmets, so that they were effective protection.

MISH MASH

You can alter the finished look of papier-mâché pulp (mash) in a number of ways. You can start out with a finer pulp by chopping up the paper in the blender for a longer time. You can also sand the dried pulp with sandpaper to change the look.

The color of the pulp can also be varied. You can simply use colored paper scraps when you start out (try adding some colored tissue paper—it "bleeds" freely), or you can dye the pulp with fabric dyes (be sure to protect your hands with rubber gloves). Add a little liquid dye to the pulp and work it in with your hands. Keep in mind the color will be lighter when dry. Experiment by combining some dyed pulp with some undyed pulp for a mottled look.

A-TISKET A-TASKET

This woven salt dough basket is surprisingly tough. With normal care it will hold up for many years. Use it to hold rolls and sliced bread at the dinner table or odds and ends around the house.

SALT DOUGH BASKET

Salt dough (see page 81)
Bread pan
Cooking oil
Rolling pin
Ruler
Knife
Varnish

Note You can use any ovenproof pan or bowl as a frame for this basket. Use it inverted as described in the instructions or form your basket in the inside of the pan or bowl.

1. Have the salt dough ready. Most dough baskets require about half a batch of dough as made on page 81.

2. Turn the bread pan upside down. Rub cooking oil all over the outside.

3. Roll the salt dough out about ¼″ thick. (Sprinkle a little flour on your work surface, if it is sticking.) Cut the dough into ¾″ strips using the ruler and the knife.

4. Lay 5 or 6 strips across the bread pan as shown.

Then lay 2 or 3 strips lengthwise, weaving them over and under the crosspieces.

Weave two strips around the sides of the pan. Hold the strips in place by wetting the dough with a very small amount of water where two strips meet. Press the dough together firmly but gently. If your strips are not long enough to go all the way around the sides, splice them together. Join the new strip right next to the old, preferably under a crossing strip for added stability.

Splice at crossing strip

5. Cut the excess off all the strips at the lip of the bread pan. Roll some dough into a long rope and wind it around the pan right at the lip. Moisten the ends of the strips to help them stick to the dough rope.

6. Let the basket dry at room temperature (this takes about 3 days), or bake it in a 325°F oven for about an hour. Let cool completely before carefully

Baskets are made from every imaginable material. Most are made from cane and reed, but they can be made from everything from pine needles to cloth coils. While many former handcrafts are now machine-made, baskets continue to be made only by hand.

▶

The oldest known baskets were unearthed in Faiyum, Egypt. They are thought to be between 10,000 and 12,000 years old.

lifting the dough basket off the bread pan.

7. Seal the basket with a coat of varnish to strengthen it and protect it from moisture. Brush on an acrylic varnish or spray the basket with artists' fixative.

Tip Give the basket a textured look by poking holes in the soft dough with a toothpick or the tines of a fork. Experiment with other textures using other utensils.

Give the basket a golden-brown color by brushing it with

a beaten egg yolk mixed with a little water before baking it in the oven.

HOT SPOT

Cloth-covered craft cord or rope can be shaped into circles, ovals, and even baskets. This simple circle made from cord and torn fabric strips makes a perfect trivet for hot dishes.

Some trivets are three-legged iron stands. That's what the *tri* in trivet stands for— three, like the *tri* in triangle, tripod, and triple.

CLOTH COIL TRIVET

1/2" craft cord or rope, about 7 feet long
1/4 yard cotton or cotton-blend fabric
Scissors

Note Fabric stores carry 1/4" and 1/2" craft cord made for covering with fabric, but you can also use thick, lightweight rope. Seven feet of 1/2" cord makes a circular trivet about 7 1/2" in diameter.

1. Cut each end of the cord at an angle.

Cut at an angle

2. Tear the fabric into 1" strips. Do this by cutting slits an inch apart at one end of the fabric and tearing the fabric at each slit.

3. Place one end of a fabric strip along one end of the cord, as shown. Reverse direction and wrap the strip around the cord. As you wrap, overlap each previous strip so that no cord shows.

4. When you have wrapped about 4" of cord, bend the wrapped portion into a tight circle. Secure it in place by wrapping the fabric strip in a figure-eight that loops through the circle and back out to the yet unwrapped portion of the cord.

5. Continue wrapping the cord and coiling it, holding the coils in place with figure-eight twists every 2 or 3 inches. When you have used up one fabric strip, wrap the start of another under

the last few inches of the first, and continue.

6. Finish the coil by wrapping the tapered end of the cord together with the previous coil, as if they

were one. Pull the end of the strip through the final wraps and trim off the end.

Tip You can thread the end of the fabric strip through a large-eye tapestry needle to help you pull the strip between the coils.

Variations on a Theme
Change colors as you coil by using different colored strips. Experiment with different shapes. Make an oval trivet by shaping the first bend in the cord into an oval. Make a basket by coiling straight up, angling out the coils a little as each circle is completed.

Many North American Indians make coil baskets. Intricate designs are incorporated into the baskets as they take shape.

HANDLE WITH CARE

Weaving is easy with a simple frame loom you can make yourself. Use torn fabric strips to make thick, cushiony potholders. With this same technique, you can also weave placemats, handbags, and even rugs.

WOVEN RAG POTHOLDER

Cotton or cotton-blend fabric, about ½ yard
Cotton yarn or thin string
Medium-weight yarn
Paper, about 8½″ × 11″
Flat stick, such as a stir stick used for painting
Frame loom (see page 134)

Note The instructions here are for a potholder measuring about 7″ square. Make yours larger (or smaller) by changing the number of warp threads on your loom.

1. Tear the fabric into 1″ strips. Do this by cutting slits at one end of the fabric an inch apart and tearing the fabric at each slit.

2. Wrap cotton thread around the loom as described in *Frame Loom* on page 134. Wrap enough yarn to make 28 warp threads.

Wrap 28 warp threads

Weaving is closely related to basketry. The main difference is the need for a loom, because the fibers used for weaving cloth and tapestries are more flexible than the fibers used in making baskets.

▶

The Story of Art
Perhaps the most famous woven tapestry is the one popularly known as the Bayeux Tapestry after the name of the town where it was discovered. It is actually a woven strip decorated with embroidery, illustrating William the Conqueror's invasion of England in 1066. The piece is 20″ wide and an incredible 230 feet long! It is not known who made the tapestry, nor how long it took.

3. Place the piece of paper over the warp threads that are wrapped around the back of the loom to block them from view. (This makes it a lot easier to concentrate on the warp threads you're working with.) Slip the painter's stir stick under the warp threads at the front of the loom.

4. Wrap about 12 feet of medium-weight yarn into a small bundle. Weave about 3″ of the loose end through the warp threads. Now weave over and under the warp threads from side to side. Push the yarn down against the stir stick with your fingers, each time you reach a side. To prevent the far warp threads from being pulled inward, gently arch the yarn before you push it down.

Weave about a 1″ band with this yarn.

5. Wrap about 9 feet of cotton yarn into a bundle, and weave a narrow band (¼″–½″) with it. Start the weaving the same way you did the medium-weight yarn; finish it by back-weaving the last few inches.

6. Now weave with the torn fabric strips. Start and finish as before. Fold the strips in half to make them a little more manageable. When you finish with one strip, simply continue with another (overlap them slightly so there aren't any gaps). Continue until the weaving is about 7″ long. End with another narrow band of cotton yarn.

8. Cut the warp threads about 2″ beyond the end of the potholder. Cut them the same distance from the beginning. Remove the medium-weight yarn that was woven at the start. Knot the warp threads together right up close to the narrow bands at either end of the potholder. Trim the excess with a pair of scissors.

Tip Weave another potholder (or another item) on the reverse side of the loom *before* you cut the warp threads, if you like. Block off the first weaving with a piece of paper to make it easier to see what you're doing.

Variations on a Theme
Experiment with different materials. You can weave with just yarn, of course, to create some striking tapestries and useful articles. You can also incorporate such things as feathers, straw, and twigs into woven pieces to make them three-dimensional.

Experiment with changing the over-and-under pattern. Instead of always weaving over one warp thread and under another, try going over two and under one, for instance. Play around with changing colors in the middle of a row, and weaving shapes into your tapestries.

FRAME LOOM

Frame looms are among the easiest to use and to make. There are several types of frame loom. The version shown here has notches at either end to hold the warp threads, although you can also tap in a row of tiny nails (take care the wood doesn't split).

Make your loom out of pine (have a lumberyard rip 1″ × 3″ pine boarding down the middle) or from an old picture frame or stretcher strips. A 12″ × 18″ frame is a good size to start with. If you are using pine, saw the wood into four pieces and attach them at right angles with corner braces or irons. If you are using an old frame or stretcher strips, reinforce the frame at the corners.

Carefully measure and mark lines ¼″ apart on both ends of the frame. Use a thick knife blade (such as a pocketknife blade) to make a notch at each mark.

Make notches every ¼″

All woven pieces are made up of the *warp* (the threads that run vertically, and are usually hidden) and the *weft* (the horizontal yarn or fabric strips that are woven in and out of the warp). Warping the frame loom is very simple. It is best to use a strong material such as cotton crochet yarn or other

thin but strong string. Wrap the string from one end of the loom to the other, pressing the string into the notches to keep the warp evenly spaced. A notched frame loom can be woven on both sides (one at a time), or the extra warp threads can be cut away and discarded when you are done weaving just one side of the loom.

WARP THREADS

The oldest picture of a loom is on a pottery dish that was found in a tomb at El Badari, Egypt. The dish is thought to date from about 4400 B.C.

NIGHT LIGHT

The candlelight shining through the holes of this tin can lantern makes an interesting pattern on walls and ceilings. Make several lanterns for an even more dramatic effect.

PIERCED TIN CAN LANTERN

| Empty metal food can (with removable paper label) |
| Permanent marker |
| Assorted nails |
| Hammer |
| Towel |

Note Look for cans that have plain sides without any ridges. These make the nicest lanterns.

1. Remove the label from the can. Scrape any remaining glue off the can by chipping it off with a knife while holding the can under running cold water.

2. Draw a pattern of dots on the outside of the can with the perma-

nent marker (be careful not to smudge the dots before the ink dries). Use the patterns shown here, or come up with your own ideas.

Indoor lighting probably originated about 50,000 years ago when Cro-Magnon man placed a fiber wick in a saucer-like depression that held animal fat.

▶

The earliest use of the metallic element tin was in Mesopotamia about 3500 B.C. Today tin is chiefly used in making tin plate. Tin cans are actually tin-plated sheet iron.

3. Fill the can with water and place it in the freezer. Leave for at least 24 hours in order to freeze solid.

4. Place the can on its side on a folded towel. Use the assorted nails to pierce through the pattern of dots you've drawn. Hammer the nails in just far enough to pierce the metal. Return the can to the freezer for a few hours, if the ice is melting too quickly.

5. When you are done, place the can in the sink and let the ice

melt. Dry the lantern (take care not to cut or scratch yourself on the jagged edges inside the can), place a small candle in it, and light. (Have an adult help you with lighting the candle.)

Variations on a Theme
Pierce a pattern of holes in the metal top from a frozen juice can (the kind that is held in place with a plastic strip that has nice, smooth edges) to make a hanging ornament. Place the lid on a wooden work surface you can bang nails into, such as a scrap

of soft pine. Hang several pierced lids together in front of a light source for a dramatic nighttime mobile.

You can also pierce holes in paper. Make your own note cards or lamp shades using this technique. Place the paper on top of a piece of foam or several layers of felt. Poke the holes with a sharp needle, taking care to space them evenly.

THE ARTFUL DODGER

This whimsical snake will liven up a room while keeping cold drafts at bay. It's also hefty enough to keep doors propped open, or it can be used as a book end when it's coiled.

Did you know?
Warm air is constantly being drawn towards colder air. When your parents warn you not to let in any cold air, they really mean not to let any warm air out.

DRAFT STOPPER

¼ yard tightly-woven fabric, such as cotton or a cotton-blend
Fabric paints or acrylics
Sand, about 2 shovelfuls
Needle and thread
Funnel

Note A 36″ snake spans most doorways. Make your snake longer, if your doors are wider than usual.

1. Fold the fabric in half lengthwise. Make a mark 37″ from one end; cut off the excess fabric. (If you are using 36″ fabric, omit this step.) Round off the corners at one end for the head; taper the fabric slightly at the other end for the tail.

CUTTING LINE

2. Open up the fabric and lay it on some newspaper. Paint it to look like a snake (remember the top of the snake is where the fabric was folded). Paint crazy patterns in bright colors or make the snake more realistic looking. Let dry.

3. Fold the fabric in half again, this time with the painted side facing in. Sew the fabric together leaving a 1/2" seam. Leave an opening at the tail end. Turn the fabric right-side out.

4. Place the funnel in the tail end of the snake and pour in enough sand to fill out the snake's form. Sew the tail opening shut.

Variations on a Theme
You can stuff your snake with fiberfill instead of sand, if you don't plan on using it as a draft stopper.

Embellish the snake with buttons and other decorative trims for a different look.

Add some felt legs to your snake to turn it into a caterpillar. Turn it into a "bookworm" with a pair of glasses painted at one end!

CASE CLOSED

This ingenious cushion cover for a round pillow is so easy to make that you can re-cover your cushions whenever you like. The cover is folded and tied in place instead of being sewn.

FOLDED CUSHION COVER

Round pillow or pillow form
Felt, about 1¼ yards of 72" felt
Measuring tape
String
Needle and strong thread

Note One-and-one-quarter yards of felt will cover a 16" round pillow that is about 4" thick. For a larger pillow (or one that is plumper), use a longer piece of felt.

1. Place the end of the measuring tape in the center of the pillow and measure from there to the center of the other side.

measure from center of one side to center of other side

2. Spread the piece of felt out flat on a firm surface. Cut a piece of string 2" longer than the measurement you made in step 1. Tie the string to a felt-tip marker. Holding the end of the

piece of string in the very center of the piece of felt, pull the string taut and carefully draw a circle on the felt. (You may find this is easier to do with two people—one to hold the end of the string, the other to draw the circle.)

In ancient Greece and Rome, cushions and pillows were the only form of upholstery in homes.

▶

There was a time when only the very wealthiest people slept with soft pillows. Throughout history, however, hard pillows were sometimes preferred because they were thought to be better for your health. The ancient Chinese slept with their heads elevated in porcelain "cradles."

3. Cut out the circle. Fold the circle in half. Thread the needle with the strong thread and tie an 8″ length to either end of the fold.

Tie threads here

Open the circle and refold it in the opposite direction; tie thread to both ends of that fold. Unfold and refold the circle two more times, so that there are 8 pieces of thread evenly spaced around the circle.

4. Place the pillow in the center of the circle. Tie together any two pieces of thread that are opposite one another. Knot them securely. Now bring together and tie the pair of threads that are in the opposite direction.

Tie these strings first

Then tie these strings

Knot the remaining two pairs of thread. Arrange and smooth out the folds.

Tip Sew a button in the center of the pillow to hide the knots, if you like.

Variations on a Theme

You can cover a square pillow with a similar technique. Measure around the pillow starting and ending at the very center of one side. Cut a square out of felt that is that size.

Tie the strong thread to each corner of the felt square, and to the mid-point on each side. Place the pillow in the center of the felt square. Bring two opposite mid-point threads together and knot them; do the same with the other mid-point threads.

Knot opposite sides together

At one time, there were as many as 20 different spellings of the word "pillow" in English. Among them: plye, pele, pilewe, and pylow.

Pull the four corners of the felt square out, folding them to look like a pinwheel.

Turn the pillow over and tie the threads of the opposite corners together.

Knot opposite corners together

The phrase "to consult with one's pillow" was once a common expression. It meant to take a night to consider a matter of importance—in other words, "to sleep on it."

FRAMED!

Special artwork and cherished photographs deserve to be framed. Here are two simple frames without glass that you can make. Use them to frame some of your own work or give them as gifts.

FOAM–CORE FRAME

Paper, 8½″ × 11″
Scissors
Foam-core board, about 8½″ × 11″
X-acto knife
Blunt tool, such as the end of a paintbrush
Metallic paint
Clear acetate (optional)

Note The frame shown here is an ornate old-fashioned looking oval. Make your frame any shape and style using the same technique.

1. Make a template for the frame's outline and opening. Fold the 8½″ × 11″ paper in half, and in half again. Draw two curved lines on the paper, making sure the folds are on the left-hand side and bottom, as shown.

Make the frame outline scalloped as it is here or any way you like. Cut along the two lines. Open the paper.

2. Lay the template on the piece of foam-core board. Trace around the outline and the opening. Cut along these lines with the X-acto knife. Hold the knife as straight as possible to make the cuts level.

3. With the blunt end of a paint-brush or other tool, "draw" patterns and designs on the frame as decoration. Go over the lines if necessary to make them deep enough to really stand out. Make rows of dots by gently pushing the end of the paintbrush straight down (take care not to push too hard or you might break through the board).

4. Paint the frame with metallic paints. Spray paint is best for over-all painting (be sure to get the edges); brush on the kind of paint that comes in a jar to further emphasize the incised lines. Let dry.

Tip Protect whatever you are framing with a piece of clear ace-tate cut slightly larger than the frame's opening. Tape it to the inside of the front of the frame.

The Story of Art
The first paintings were painted directly on walls and ceilings. Artists often "framed" them with painted lines to give them definition and a finished look. When paintings became portable (when they were done on canvas or wood), frames were used not only to enhance them, but also to act as a deterrent to thieves.

▶

Tricks of the Trade

Consider your artwork carefully when you choose a frame for it (homemade and store-bought alike). A frame should complement, but not overwhelm, a drawing or painting. Choose simple wooden or metal strip frames for abstract pieces, for instance. More ornate frames are more in keeping with classic still lifes and portraits.

Choose your mat board in a color that complements the art, as well. Pick up one of the colors in the art itself, or choose a neutral shade such as off-white or beige.

PAPER–COVERED FRAME

| Sturdy cardboard, 2 pieces about 8½" × 11" plus a 2" × 7" piece |
| Wrapping paper or art paper |
| Medium-weight paper, about 2" × 8" |
| X-acto knife |
| Rubber cement |
| White glue |

Note The instructions here are for an 8½" × 11" frame. Alter the dimensions of all the materials to suit any other frame size.

1. Draw the outline of an opening 2" in from all sides on one of the pieces of cardboard. Cut out the opening with the X-acto knife.

2. Cut two pieces of 10½" × 13" wrapping paper. Place one piece face down. Brush rubber cement over the entire back of the paper and on one side of the cut out frame. Let dry; then carefully position the frame in the center of the paper.

1.

2.

Rub your hands over the frame to bond the paper to the cardboard and to smooth out any wrinkles.

3. With the X-acto knife, cut an "X" in the frame's opening, from corner to corner. Trim the paper at the outer corners.

Cut "X"

Trim corners

Fold the flaps back around the opening; glue them down (brush some rubber cement to the back of the frame where the flaps touch). Glue down the excess paper around the frame.

Trim excess

4. Cover the other 8½" × 11" piece of cardboard with the remaining piece of wrapping paper.

5. Lay the two pieces of cardboard end to end, face down. With the white glue, glue the 2" × 8" paper strip so that it spans the two pieces as shown.

PAPER STRIP

Let dry; fold the frame at this "hinge."

6. Cut one piece of wrapping paper 4" × 9", and one 1¾" × 6¾". Cover the 2" × 7" strip of cardboard with the larger paper. Use the smaller piece to cover the flaps on the back side. This is the support to hold up the frame.

7. Score a line 1½" from the top of the support with the X-acto knife. Bend it back slightly. Glue it to the mid-point of the back of the frame with white glue. Let dry.

BACK OF FRAME

1½"

8. Lift the front of the frame and position your artwork so that it shows through the opening. Tape the artwork to the frame back. Lower the front of the frame and adjust the angle of the support, so that the frame stands on its own.

EYE OF THE BEHOLDER

The way people dress throughout the world is as varied as the languages that are spoken. While some fashions come and go, many clothes are designed with climate and function in mind and change little over the years. Traditional clothes such as these go back a long, long time.

In some cultures, such as our own, there are few rules of dress, and clothing is a form of self-expression. Fashions borrow freely from various periods in history as well as from other cultures. Such clothing really is wearable art!

GOTCHA COVERED!

Not all art is messy, but in the excitement of discovering new techniques and things to make you can sometimes forget what you're doing. It's a good idea to wear a cover-all of some sort, because, if nothing else, it makes cleaning up that much easier.

The smock gets its name from *smock frock,* a yoked shirt or loose blouse made from coarse linen that was worn by field laborers in Europe. Originally it was smocked, a method of pleating and stitching fabric in a honeycomb design that cinches in the fullness of a garment at the yoke and cuffs.

OVERSIZED SHIRT SMOCK

Man's long-sleeved button-front shirt
¼″ elastic, 2 pieces 8″ long
Large-eye tapestry needle
Needle and thread
Fabric paint or acrylics

Note Ask your dad if he has an old shirt that's too worn to mend. Even clothes can be recycled!

1. Put on the shirt. Stand up straight with your arms hanging by your side. Have someone cut off the sleeves about 2″ below the tips of your fingers.

Cut 2″ below tips of fingers →

2. Take off the shirt and turn it inside out. Turn back 1″ at the bottom of one sleeve. Sew around the sleeve to make a ¾″ casing for the elastic. Leave a 2″ opening.

Leave 2″ opening

3. Thread the elastic through the large-eye needle and insert it in the casing. Take care not to pull it all the way through. Adjust the elastic so that it fits snugly around your wrist; sew the ends together.

Sews ends of elastic together

4. Sew the opening in the casing closed. Insert the elastic in the other sleeve in the same way.

5. Turn the shirt right-side out and decorate with paint. Make large free-hand brush marks all over the shirt, or spatter it with paint in an over-all pattern. (Put it in a large cardboard box if you are spatter-painting, to protect yourself and your work area from spatters.) Let dry.

Variations on a Theme
Instead of sewing casings for the elastic, you can simply tie the elastic into tight bands to slip over the ends of the shirt sleeves to keep them from flapping about.

Many professions require protective clothing. Cooks, for instance, wear aprons (so do carpenters, but theirs are meant as holders rather than as protective garb). Scientists wear lab coats. What other cover-all garments can you think of?

I ♥ FOOD

TO A TEE

These cheerful T-shirts are as sunny as summer itself. With fiber-reactive dyes, you can tie-dye shirts in as many colors as you like. Best of all, you don't even need a stove—this type of dyeing is done in cold water.

TIE-DYE T-SHIRT

White, or light-colored, 100% cotton T-shirt
Fiber-reactive dyes, 2 or more colors (see page 144)
Fixer solution (see page 144)
Rubber bands, about 4
Rubber gloves
Plastic sheet (see *Note*)
Plastic bag, 1-gallon size

Note Protect your work table with a plastic sheet or a couple of plastic garbage bags opened up and overlapped on the table. (Save these bags to use again whenever you need to protect your work surface.)

1. Wash the shirt in warm, soapy water; rinse well. (You must do this even if your shirt is new, to remove any sizing that might affect the fabric's ability to accept dye.) Place the shirt in the container of fixer solution. Let soak 30 minutes.

2. Remove the shirt from the fixer; wring it out. Lay the shirt on the plastic-covered table. Smooth out the big wrinkles and bumps.

3. Fold or gather the shirt to create the pattern of your choice. To make stripes, like on the shirt shown here, fold the shirt from hem to neckline in inch-wide accordion folds (back and forth folds).

Evenly space four rubber bands around the bundle to keep it in place.

4. Set the bundle on its side. Put on the rubber gloves to protect your hands. Dribble a little dye along the fold lines—use a differ-ent color for each fold, or dye each section of the bundle a different color.

Place bundle on its side

Turn the bundle over and do the same on the other side.

5. Place the bundle in the plastic bag. Leave it for 1 to 3 days (the longer you let the dyes set, the brighter the colors).

6. Remove the bundle from the plastic bag. Rinse it under running water until the water is nearly clear. Remove the rubber bands. Rinse a few minutes more under running water.

7. Fill the sink with a squirt of dishwashing liquid and the hot-test water from the tap. Put the shirt into the sink; let soak for 10 minutes. Rinse in clean water until

▶

Tie-dyeing originated in the Orient around the 6th century. It is still commonly used to decorate fabrics in such places as India, Africa, Japan, China, and various Southeast Asian countries.

Make diagonal stripes by folding the shirt diagonally.

Most people agree that T-shirts get their name from their shape. Some historians, however, feel that the name comes from the "tea shirts" worn by 17th century dock workers in Maryland. They wore the special shirts to keep loose tea leaves from collecting under their collars when they were unloading the ships.

the water runs clear. Wring out the shirt and lay flat to dry.

Variations on a Theme

Traditionally, tie-dyeing was done in one color using hot water dye. You can do it this way yourself, too.

Get a dye bath ready (using a dye such as Rit®) following the instructions on the package. Crumple, fold, twist, knot or stitch the fabric, binding it together tightly with rubber bands, string, or a needle and thread. Wherever you bind the fabric, no dye can penetrate. Dye the fabric, then cut away the bindings and open it up to reveal the pattern you have created.

FIBER–REACTIVE DYES & FIXER

Fiber-reactive dye is available at many fabric and yarn stores, as well as art and craft suppliers. It is sold in both powdered and liquid form, often in small amounts that include a separate packet of fixer.

Follow the directions on the package or use this general rule. One teaspoon of powdered dye is enough to make ½ cup of dye solution. Place the dye in a disposable container, and add 1 tablespoon warm water to the container; stir with a Popsicle stick to make a thick paste. Pour in the rest of the water.

Dyes can be mixed together to create new colors. Covered, they can be stored for several weeks in a cool, dark place.

Make a fixer solution from a chemical called sodium carbonate (not to be confused with sodium bicarbonate, which is baking soda), salt, and water. (If you can't find sodium carbonate where you purchased your dyes, you can buy it from a swimming pool chemical supplier. Ask for soda ash or sal soda.) Mix 4 teaspoons sodium carbonate and ¼ cup salt per shirt in a bucket. Add enough water to cover the shirt completely.

Handle these chemicals with care. It's a good idea to wear rubber gloves whenever you are working with dye (and put on a smock, too, in case of splashes). Measure the powdered dyes carefully, so you don't send the fine particles flying. When dyeing, use only disposable containers or old pots and jars reserved only for dyeing purposes.

Make a sunburst on your shirt. Start with the shirt flat; pinch the fabric near the center of the shirt; lift up. Twist the shirt into a tight spiral, then roll it into a doughnut shape. Place a rubber band around the outside to hold it in place. Dribble dye on the top; then turn the bundle over and do the same on the other side. Proceed as usual.

WHAT A CINCH

Long belts that tie are perfect for cinching in costumes as well as wearing with "real" clothes. Here are two belts you can make yourself. The first is braided from long pieces of yarn; the second uses a technique known as spool knitting.

BRAIDED BELT

Yarn in assorted colors, 24 strands about 10 feet long

Scissors

Note Use as many colors as you like. The belt shown here uses 4 different colors (6 strands of each) which produce a nice, colorful effect.

1. Tie the strands of yarn together, with a loose knot, about 20″ from one end. Anchor the yarn in a drawer by placing the yarn—up to the knot—in the drawer and closing it as far as it will go.

2. Divide the yarn into 3 sections of 8 strands each. Loosely knot the ends of these 3 bundles of strands. Braid the 3 bundles of strands until the braided part measures about 48″, or about twice the measurement around your waist.

THREE-STRAND BRAID

As you braid the long strands, stop and shake the yet-to-be-braided yarn every few inches or so. The extra yarn has a way of getting tangled as you braid; shaking the strands loose makes the job a lot easier.

3. Remove the yarn from the drawer and untie the knot holding all the strands together. Double over the braided part and join the two ends by wrapping yarn around them as tightly as possible. Tie this yarn to itself to keep it from unraveling.

wrap yarn around ends

4. Loop the belt around a chair. Finish off the belt by braiding the loose strands into small braids (using 3 pairs of strands per braid). Choose the colors for these small braids randomly, or pair off the strands of any one braid in 3 colors. Tie the end of each braid with a secure knot. Trim the excess yarn evenly with the scissors.

EIGHT SMALL BRAIDS

5. To wear the belt, place it around your waist and slip the wrapped portion through the loop.

Belts come in all sorts of styles. Some are threaded through belt loops of trousers and skirts. Wider sashes are simply tied around the waist. Still others go over the shoulders and clip on to whatever they are holding up. We call this last type suspenders, of course!

▶

Spool-knitting is perhaps more closely related to macrame than to the knitting that is done with long needles. Both macrame and hand knitting are ancient crafts.

SPOOL-KNITTED BELT

Yarn, 1 or more colors, about 60–75 feet
Knitting spool (see below)
Blunt tapestry needle

Note This belt, which measures 36″, is meant to be tied with a loose knot. Make your belt longer (or shorter), if you want to tie it differently.

1. Drop one end of the yarn through the hole in the spool. Let about 6″ hang below the bottom of the spool.

2. Loop the yarn around each nail once. This is what the loops should look like from above.

3. Loop the yarn over the first nail again. Slip the first loop up and over this second loop, letting the first loop come right off the nail completely.

Lift first loop up + over second loop

Continue doing this all the way around the spool (be sure to follow the order of the original loops). Every few rounds, pull on the yarn that is hanging through the hole to keep the knitting from bunching up inside the spool.

4. Change colors by cutting the yarn you are using and tying on a new color. Trim the excess yarn near the knot. The knot itself will be hidden in the knitted cord.

5. Keep knitting the belt until it is the desired length. Finish off by cutting the yarn about 6″ from the top of the spool. Slip the loops off the nails one at a time, carefully pulling the yarn through each loop. Make a final knot.

Variations on a Theme
Spool-knitted cord can be made into all sorts of items. Coil a long piece to make a trivet (sew it together as you coil it). Make a necklace using metallic thread. Fashion some miniature rugs for a dollhouse.

KNITTING SPOOL

To make your own knitting spool you need an empty wooden thread spool, 4 finish nails (these are the kind that have no heads) and a hammer.

Carefully nail the nails into one end of the spool, spacing them evenly around the hole. Leave the nails sticking up about 1/2″. These are the posts you wrap the yarn or string around as you knit the cord.

Just call me Nancy!

European children enjoy making spool-knitted items using a purchased tool that has a face painted on it. It is affectionately known as Knitting Nancy.

DYED IN THE WOOL

Make the belts described on pages 145 and 146 from yarn that you've dyed yourself using natural dyes. Natural dyes yield subtle colors quite different from chemical dyes. The process is easy to do and a lot of fun.

Gather a variety of dyestuffs, from your kitchen as well as from outdoors. Onion skins, herbs and spices, nutshells, and vegetables such as beets all yield dyes, as do flower blossoms, the leaves, berries, and bark of trees, and lichen. If you divide a skein of wool (use 100 percent wool, because it takes dye better than cotton or synthetic fibers) into small hanks, you can experiment with all sorts of dyestuffs and have plenty of different colored yarn on hand to weave, knit, and craft with. To form hanks, wind some yarn

around your outstretched fingers in a figure-eight and tie loosely in two spots with a short piece of yarn.

You'll get the best results if you first mordant your wool to make it fade-resistant. Alum is one of the most common chemicals used as a mordant. The day before you plan on dyeing (or well before, in which case let the mordanted wool dry), fill an old pot with enough water to cover all the yarn, and add 4 ounces of alum mixed with 1 ounce cream of tartar. Bring to a boil and cook for one hour. Let cool overnight in the mordant bath.

Look for alum at your local pharmacy. Cream of tartar can be found in the spice section of your supermarket.

The next day, boil up your plants or kitchen scraps to extract the dye. For the small amounts of yarn you are going to dye, you only need a couple of handfuls of dyestuffs for each color. Put the plants and a little water into another old pot. Simmer for about 30 minutes. Strain the dye and put it back into the pot with enough cold water to cover the yarn you are dyeing.

Place the pot on the stove. Poking the yarn gently with a spoon, cook until it turns the shade you want (remember the yarn will look lighter when it's dry). Let the yarn cool in the pot. Rinse it with cool water until the rinse water runs clear. Gently squeeze the yarn and hang it to dry in a shady spot.

Here are some plants you can use as dyestuffs. Using alum as the mordant, these are the colors they yield.

Dandelion flowers—Yellow

Elderberries—Violet

Marigolds—Yellow-tan

Nettles—Greenish yellow

Red onion skins—Reddish orange

Yellow onion skins—Yellow to burnt orange

TREAD SOFTLY

No one really knows when our ancestors first made footwear, but it is likely that the shoes were similar to many of the moccasins still made by Native Americans today. Make your own pair of soft-soled moccasins from felt using a traditional Iroquois design.

Did you know?
The word *moccasin* comes from an Algonquin Indian name for footwear.

CENTER–SEAM MOCCASINS

Paper, about 11″ × 14″
Felt-tip marker
Scissors
Measuring tape
Felt, about ½ yard 72″ felt
Stitch Witchery®, about ¾ yard
Iron
Needle and embroidery thread

1. Place one of your feet (with or without socks) on a separate piece of paper and trace around it. Cut out the tracing.

2. Wrap the measuring tape around the widest part of your foot. Make a note of the measurement.

Measure around widest part

3. On the large sheet of paper draw a pattern for one of the moccasins. It should look like the diagram below. Use the foot tracing to help you determine the size. Trace around it right-side up for one foot; flop it over for the other foot. Make the distance from the outside of one foot to the outside of the other equal the measurement you made with the tape.

Add ½″ at toe

Make this equal to measurement made in step 2

2″

Add ⅝″ allowance at heel

Add ½″ at the top of the moccasin, and ⅝″ at the heel, as shown. Note the other measure-

ments in the diagram. Cut the pattern out along the outline.

4. Set the iron on "wool." Cut two 18″ × 24″ pieces of felt. Sandwich the Stitch Witchery® between the felt. Following the manufacturer's directions, iron the felt pieces together to bond them. Let cool.

5. Place the pattern on the felt and trace around it with the felt-tip marker (make two tracings, one for each moccasin). Cut the two moccasins out.

6. Fold one felt piece in half. Sew the front half with a whip stitch, spacing the stitches about ¼″ apart.

Space stitches ¼″ apart

FOLD

Sew the back of the moccasin the same way.

7. Turn the moccasin inside out. Fold down the side flaps and try it on for size. Make the other moccasin in the same way.

Variations on a Theme
Make these moccasins out of leather, if you like. Follow the instructions above with one exception—don't bother to bond two pieces of leather together. A single layer will do.

To whip stitch the felt for these moccasins, place the raw edges of the felt together and sew them with diagonal stitches that go right over the edge, as shown here.

Stitch Witchery® is the brand name of an iron-on bonding mesh. Ask for it at a fabric store or in the sewing section of a department store.

FIT TO BE TIED

The country of Java is famous for its fine batiks. These wax-resist-decorated fabrics have a very distinctive look. You can create your own using a much simplified method. Start small and make a scarf or panel for a wall-hanging.

BATIK SCARF

White 100% cotton fabric, about 16″ square
Newspaper
Waxed paper
Paraffin, one slab
Double-boiler
Old paintbrush
Liquid Rit® dyes, 2 or more colors
Rubber gloves
Bucket
Iron
Needle and thread

Note The scarf shown here is dyed with two colors, red and blue. The completed scarf is white (the color of the fabric), red, and purple (red and blue make purple). When you choose your colors, keep in mind how they mix to make new colors.

1. Put a thick layer of newspaper on your work surface. Lay waxed paper over this. Place the fabric on the waxed paper (it should be washed—and dried—to remove any sizing that might affect the dyeing).

2. Prepare the first dye. You should always start with the lightest color. (Using one bucket, you can make one dye bath now, then clean out the bucket and make the other while the fabric is drying from the first dyeing.) Mix a gallon of hot tap water with ¼ cup liquid dye and 1 tablespoon salt in a bucket. Stir well; let cool.

1 GALLON WATER + ¼ CUP DYE + 1 TABLESPOON SALT

3. Place the paraffin in the top of the double boiler. Heat it over boiling water until it melts. (*Caution:* Paraffin can ignite. Be sure to ask an adult to help you here.) Watch it carefully so that it doesn't overheat. Remove the double-boiler from the stove. ▶

You can also use a pre-hemmed man's cotton handkerchief for this project.

Experiment with various light-colored fabrics for different effects.

The Story of Art

While many countries decorate fabric with a wax-resist technique, the batiks of Java are the best known. The Javanese invented a tool called a tjanting (CHAHN-ting) that allows the artisans to make very fine lines with the liquid wax. Traditionally, Javanese batiks were made in three colors—the creamy, off-white color of the fabric (made by soaking it in coconut oil), dark blue (from indigo) and brown (from soga bark). Today many other colors are used, as well.

4. With the melted wax, paint the part of your design that is meant to stay the color of the fabric. (You can sketch a design on the fabric with a piece of chalk first, if you like, or paint freehand.) The wax should saturate the fabric for best results. Reheat the paraffin if it starts to solidify. Let the wax harden on the fabric.

5. Put the fabric in the dye bath. Make sure it is completely immersed. Leave it there for 30 min-

utes, or until it is a little darker than you want (it will dry lighter).

6. Remove the fabric and rinse it in lukewarm water until the water runs clear (protect your hands with rubber gloves). Hang to dry. Empty the dye in the sink, clean the bucket, and mix the next dye bath.

7. When the fabric is dry, carefully reheat the wax and paint the fabric wherever you want the first color to remain.

Let the wax harden, then dye with the second color. Rinse; hang to dry. (Repeat this sequence with any additional colors.)

8. To remove the wax, place the fabric between two sheets of old newspaper (the ink is liable to rub off fresh newspaper). Iron over it with a hot, dry iron. Keep the iron moving. Replace the paper as it gets saturated with wax, and continue until no more wax is absorbed by the newspaper.

9. Wash the fabric in soapy water, as hot as you can stand it. Hang to dry. (If the fabric is still stiff with wax, have it dry cleaned.) Hem all the way around to make the edges neat.

NORTHWEST COAST

GREAT LAKES

CITIZEN BAND

These headbands can be worn by boys and girls alike. Place them on your head like an Indian head-dress, or use them to keep your hair from your face.

FELT HEADBAND
Felt strip, about 1″ × 16″
Assorted felt scraps
Sequins, buttons and other trims

¾″ elastic, about 4″ long
White glue
Needle and thread

Note The headband shown here is inspired by the feathered bands worn by a number of Indian tribes. Design your headband any way you like.

1. Cut the felt scraps into various shapes. Glue them to one side of the long felt strip, using the glue sparingly, so that it doesn't bleed through the felt.

2. Add other trims, if you like,

such as fabric trims, sequins, buttons, and beads (the latter two items you'll have to sew on).

3. Sew the elastic to the inside of the headband at both ends.

ELASTIC

Turn your headband into a tiara with the addition of lots of sparkly trims and sequins.

Instead of a felt strip, you can use a length of wide fabric trim for the background of your headband.

HATS OFF!

This unusual felt ring doesn't really look like a hat until you start twisting and folding it into various hat shapes. It's the perfect addition to your costume box because it's so many "hats" all rolled into one.

FELT CHAPEAU RING

Heavy-weight paper, about 16″ square
Black felt, about ½ yard 72″ felt
Stitch Witchery®, about 1 yard
Scissors
Iron

Note You can also use a sewing machine to stitch the layers of felt together, rather than bond them. Criss-cross the surface of the ring with stitches to make the ring fairly stiff so it will hold its shape.

1. Cut a 16″ circle out of paper (trace around a round platter or rig a compass from a pencil and piece of string—see page 137). Cut a 5″ hole in the middle of the circle. Place the ring on your head to check for size. You should be

able to pull the ring down onto your head easily. Adjust the size of the hole if necessary.

⊢— 16″ —⊣

HOLE = 5″ IN DIAMETER

The Story of Art Manipulating a felt ring to create a variety of "hats" originated in France in the 18th century. By the 1900s, chapeaugraphy ("hat-writing") was a popular entertainment in both Europe and the United States.

▶

Glass beads thought to be 4,500 years old were found in Egypt. These beads are the earliest examples of glass that have been found to date.

2. Using the paper ring as a pattern, cut three identical rings out of felt. Bond them one on top of the other, following the manufacturer's directions that come with the Stitch Witchery® (or stitch them as described in the *Note* above).

3. Place the ring on your head. Experiment by folding, twisting, and pulling the outer rim through the ring, to create various hats.

While some hats are worn as a fashion statement, most hats serve a purpose. Some are used to shade the head and keep it cool (loosely woven straw is a common material used); other hats are designed to keep the head warm (wool, fur, and down are good choices for these hats). Some hats are molded into shape with steam; others are nothing more than a long piece of cloth wrapped around the wearer's head.

BAUBLES & BEADS

People have been adorning themselves with jewelry for thousands of years. Our prehistoric ancestors probably wore necklaces strung with shell and ivory beads. You can make your own beads to string from rolled paper.

ROLLED PAPER BEAD NECKLACE

Colored paper, such as Canson paper, origami paper, and wrapping paper
Ruler
X-acto knife
White glue

Knitting needle
String or yarn
Needle

Note Rolled beads are made from narrow strips of paper that are tapered at one end and wrapped around a uniformly-thick rod. How long each strip needs to be, depends on how thick both the paper and the rod are. Make the strips longer if you are using thin paper; shorter for heavy paper.

1. The beads shown here are made from heavyweight Canson paper wrapped around a No. 9 knitting needle (you can use a pencil or a straight paint brush shaft, if you like). Cut each strip 6″ long. It should be 1″ wide at one end, tapering to ½″ at the other end.

2. Starting with the wide end, wrap the strip around the knitting needle. Squirt a small amount of glue at the beginning to hold it in place. Wrap the paper as tightly as possible, and as evenly as you can, so that the bead is built up evenly on both sides.

Finish the bead by gluing down the narrow end with a spot of glue. Hold until the glue sets.

3. String the beads on a length of string, heavy thread, or yarn.

Tip Here's a trick for making short work of cutting lots of tapered strips the same size and color.

Draw two lines on a large sheet of paper 6″ from one another. Mark the dimensions for a series of strips that alternate wide ends and narrow ends, as shown.

Cut the long straight lines at top and bottom first. Then cut each strip apart.

Laotian women often wear silver bands and coins as jewelry. These literally represent their family's wealth.

The oldest surviving jewelry that is intact dates from 2500 B.C. Necklaces, bracelets, earrings, and rings belonging to Queen Paubi of Ur, in Sumeria, were found in her burial tomb.

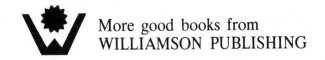

More good books from
WILLIAMSON PUBLISHING

To order additional copies of **Adventures in Art,** please enclose $12.95 per copy plus $2.50 shipping and handling. Follow "To Order" instructions on the last page. Thank you.

THE KIDS' NATURE BOOK
365 Indoor/Outdoor Activities and Experiences
by Susan Milord

Winner of the Parents' Choice Golden Award for learning and doing books, *The Kids' Nature Book* is loved by children, grandparents, and friends alike. Simple projects and activities emphasize fun while quietly reinforcing the wonder of the world we all share. Packed with facts and fun!

160 pages, 12 × 9, 425 illustrations
Quality paperback, $12.95

KIDS CREATE!
Art & Craft Experiences for 3- to 9-Year-Olds
by Laurie Carlson

What's the most important experience for children ages 3 to 9? Why to create something by themselves. Carlson provides over 150 creative experiences ranging from making dinosaur sculptures to clay cactus gardens, from butterfly puppets to windsocks. Plenty of help for the parents working with the kids, too! A delightfully innovative book.

160 pages, 11 × 8½, over 400 illustrations,
Quality paperback, $12.95

DOING CHILDREN'S MUSEUMS
A Guide to 225 Hands-On Museums
by Joanne Cleaver

Turn an ordinary day into a spontaneous "vacation" by taking a child to some of the 225 participatory children's museums, discovery rooms, and nature centers covered in this highly acclaimed, one-of-a-kind book. Filled with museum specifics to help you pick and plan the perfect place for the perfect day, Cleaver has created a most valuable resource for anyone who loves kids!

244 pages, 6 × 9,
Quality paperback, $13.95

PARENTS ARE TEACHERS, TOO
Enriching Your Child's First Six Years
by Claudia Jones

Be the best teacher your child ever has. Jones shares hundreds of ways to help any child learn in playful home situations. Lots on developing reading, writing, math skills. Plenty on creative and critical thinking, too. A book you'll love using!

192 pages, 6 × 9, illustrations,
Quality paperback, $9.95

MORE PARENTS ARE TEACHERS, TOO
Encouraging Your 6- to 12-Year-Old
by Claudia Jones

Help your children be the best they can be! When parents are involved, kids do better. When kids do better, they feel better, too. Here's a wonderfully creative book of ideas, activities, teaching methods and more to help you help your children over the rough spots and share in their growing joy in achieving. Plenty on reading, writing, math, problem-solving, creative thinking. Everything for parents who want to help but not push their children.

226 pages, 6 × 9, illustrations,
Quality paperback, $10.95

THE HOMEWORK SOLUTION
by Linda Agler Sonna

Put homework responsibilities where they belong—in the student's lap! Here it is! The simple remedy for the millions of parents who are tired of waging the never-ending nightly battle over kids' homework. Dr. Sonna's "One Step Solution" will relieve parents, kids and their siblings of the ongoing problem within a single month.

192 pages, 6 × 9,
Quality paperback, $10.95

THE BROWN BAG COOKBOOK
Nutritious Portable Lunches for Kids and Grown-Ups
by Sara Sloan

Here are more than 1,000 brown bag lunch ideas with 150 recipes for simple, quick, nutritious lunches that kids will love. Breakfast ideas, too! This popular book is now in its sixth printing!

192 pages, 8¼ × 7¼, illustrations,
Quality paperback, $9.95

Easy-to-Make
TEDDY BEARS AND ALL THE TRIMMINGS
by Jodie Davis

Now you can make the most lovable, huggable, plain or fancy teddy bears imaginable, for a fraction of store-bought costs. Step-by-step instructions and easy patterns drawn to actual size for large, soft-bodied bears, quilted bears, and even jointed bears. Plus patterns for clothes, accessories—even teddy bear furniture!

192 pages, 8½ × 11, illustrations and patterns,
Quality paperback, $13.95

GOLDE'S HOMEMADE COOKIES
by Golde Soloway

Over 50,000 copies of this marvelous cookbook have been sold. Now it's in its second edition with 135 of the most delicious cookie recipes imaginable. *Publishers Weekly* says, "Cookies are her chosen realm and how sweet a world it is to visit." You're sure to agree!

162 pages, 8¼ × 7¼, illustrations,
Quality paperback, $8.95